How ^{NOT} to Marry
the Wrong Guy

How ^{NOT} to Marry the Wrong Guy

How NOT to Marry the Wrong Guy

◆

Is He "the One"
or Should You Run?

Anne Milford *and*

Jennifer Gauvain, MSW, LCSW

Broadway Books
New York

B
BROADWAY

Copyright © 2010 by Anne Milford and Jennifer Gauvain

Library of Congress Cataloging-in-Publication Data
Milford, Anne.
How not to marry the wrong guy: is he "the one"
or should you run?/by Anne Milford and
Jennifer Gauvain.—1st ed.
p. cm.
1. Mate selection. 2. Dating (Social customs) 3. Single women.
4. Man-woman relationships. I. Gauvain, Jennifer. II. Title.
HQ801.M5665 2010
646.7'7—dc22 2009047133

ISBN 978-0-307-71875-4

PRINTED IN THE UNITED STATES OF AMERICA

Design by Donna Sinisgalli

1 3 5 7 9 10 8 6 4 2

First Edition

This book is dedicated to

all the women who shared their stories . . .

and to all the women who need to hear them.

Contents

✦

Preface

✦

It was 5 p.m. on a warm Sunday in July and my fiancé was scolding me for being late. He was upset that I was not going to have time to pack our picnic dinner for the concert that night. He stood there in a bathrobe, unshaved and unshowered, after a full day spent in front of the television. Time slowed while I reflected on my day of travel: two hours in the car to the Orlando airport, rental car return, baggage check, tedious tram ride, and the cattle call for the wide-body L-1011 aircraft jam-packed with 250 passengers. Then the whole process in reverse when I arrived in Chicago, including an hour spent in traffic getting back to his house. (Note to self: Don't most couples in love pick each other up at the airport?) I can still picture him lecturing me about how I "would never have time to go to the store and get what we need for dinner." The whole situation was so crazy that I didn't bother to mention three key things that seemed to escape him: There are no stores at thirty-five thousand feet; there was nothing I could have done to make the plane fly faster; and what the hell had he been doing all day?

I once heard a therapist use the analogy of a beach ball.

She said your problems are like a beach ball that you keep trying to hold underwater. You can try to ignore them, but eventually those problems, just like a beach ball, are going to pop up out of the water. This was the day that my beach ball finally popped out of the water. Three days later, I called off the engagement and moved back home. It was the Fourth of July—Independence Day.

When I was twenty-eight, I became engaged to a man who was completely and utterly wrong for me. For reasons that remain unclear, I fully participated in a relationship that was doomed from the start, contrary to all my gut feelings, and covered with red flags. Fortunately, I found the courage to call off the wedding before I got myself into a bigger mess.

After I ended the relationship, I moved back to my hometown, found a new job, and got an apartment. My sweet friends were worried about me and went out of their way to make sure I was doing okay. While I felt somewhat embarrassed by my poor judgment, I was so happy to be free that my joy at being back home and out of that unhealthy relationship outweighed any shame or sadness. The hardest part was facing up to the situation and making the tough call to get out.

As I talked to other women about my unfortunate engagement, I started hearing the same comments over and over. First, I was surprised by the number of women who admitted they wished they had had the courage to call off their own weddings. I even had several women (and men!) admit to short-lived first marriages that no one knew about. I also began to see a pattern develop as they started to ask me questions about my relationship. *What were the signs? How did I feel? How did I have the courage to call it off? How did my fiancé react?* I quickly realized that in many cases, they were really questioning their own relationships or pending marriages. After a while, I had mentally cataloged a collection of personal stories about doomed-from-the-start marriages, and I experienced another gut feeling: This needs to be a book. As a freelance writer, an avid reader, and a person who spends hours in bookstores and libraries, I couldn't help but notice shelves filled with rows and rows of books about how to plan a successful wedding. Countless books promise to help women "hook a man," or "find your soul mate in thirty days." Some of these books drove me crazy—women are so much smarter than this! They deserve better. What they really need is a book that helps them step back and evaluate what they want and need in a relationship.

I could have used such a book; it would have saved me a lot of heartache. That's when I had my epiphany. Who better to tell you how to extricate yourself from a dead-end relationship than a woman who has already done time in one? *No one* is better informed about unhealthy relationships than a woman who has learned the hard way. That was it! I realized that my experience of calling off a wedding could help other women. And I could uncover what a woman needs to know about marrying the *right* guy by talking to women who had married the *wrong* one! So I set out to find answers to the following:

• Why do women stay in relationships that they know are all wrong for them?

• Why do smart, talented, successful, worthy women *consciously* get engaged to the wrong guys?

- Why do they walk down that aisle even though they *already* know it is a mistake?

The first step was finding women to interview. Each woman I talked to had to meet one standard prior to being interviewed: Did she know she was making a mistake *before* she walked down the aisle? That way I knew I would be interviewing someone who (1) settled for a ho-hum (or even destructive), less-than-fulfilling relationship, and then (2) went through with her wedding even though she knew it was a mistake.

It didn't take long to find the first thirty women who fit the profile. I sent out a mass email to my friends, relatives, neighbors, and colleagues explaining the project, and I attached a questionnaire. Right away, I started receiving completed questionnaires or emails indicating that a person was willing to be interviewed. I got even more responses from people saying they knew someone who fit the criteria but they were afraid to contact her for fear of prying or being insensitive.

The amazing thing is that I didn't have to travel more than a few degrees of separation to find qualified candidates to interview. This told me I was on to something. In all cases, the women agreed to revisit personal and often painful memories to help someone else. Every single woman said something to the effect of, "If I can help prevent someone else from making the same mistake, it is worth it."

At this point in the research, I had the great fortune to begin my collaboration with Jennifer Gauvain, MSW, LCSW. Jennifer is a licensed therapist whose primary focus is helping couples and families. With more than fifteen years' experience in private practice, she helped me interpret the stories I gathered and address the issues revealed by those who forged ahead with mistaken marriages. She also shared the wisdom she and her husband of fifteen years gained while on the marriage prep team at St. Francis Xavier College Church.

After conducting the interviews and poring over the data, we discovered something remarkable. No matter what the women's background, age, education level, or religious affiliation, they all gave startlingly similar reasons for why they remained in their unfulfilling relationships or went ahead with mistaken marriages. While they were different in many ways, they all echoed the same advice: "Listen to your gut," or "Pay attention to that little voice inside of you." They talked about their gut feelings over and over, so we decided to look further into this concept.

Jennifer and I decided to track down women who *did* listen to their guts—women who had canceled weddings and ended dead-end relationships. We quickly realized that it was *much harder* to find these women. And many who we did find ultimately declined to speak to us about this time in their lives. They did not want to "go there" again and dredge up all of those painful memories. It took us a while, but we eventually conducted interviews and again found common themes and patterns in their stories. The difference was that these women were somehow able to dial in to their inner wisdom and find the courage to act on their feelings.

By presenting real-life stories, coupled with research and professional insight, we hope that a potential bride who is headed down the aisle to disaster will recognize herself and stop short before she makes a life-altering mistake. We also want to reach out to the woman who is enmeshed in an unhappy relationship simply because she doesn't want to be alone. As one woman said about her twenty-six-year-old assistant, "I wish I could bottle up all the feelings I had during my mistaken marriage and give them to her so she could see where she is headed. I have talked to her until I am blue in the face about how wrong her fiancé is for her, but she doesn't want to 'waste the six years' invested in the relationship!"

The good news is that everyone in this book went on to happy and fulfilling lives—after they ended their marriages or engagements. Their futures were not the lonely and dismal ones they had envisioned when they were in the middle of the storm. By sharing these real stories, we hope to spare others the anguish, guilt, and sadness of a failed marriage.

If you are in an unhealthy or unfulfilling relationship, we hope to help you identify what it is you are really looking for and give you ideas about how to find it. As Robert Frost eloquently said, "The best way out is always through." The stories you are about to read are true. Our hope is that by reading them, a part of you—that part of you that has been *longing* to be heard—will recognize yourself and be triggered to act. This is your opportunity to finally listen to what you *already* know is true. Through these stories, you will find your way out.

Introduction:
The Best-Kept Secret at the Wedding

Picture yourself as a bride. You are minutes away from saying "I do," but you really want to scream, "No, no, I don't!" Your heart is racing and you've got butterflies in your stomach—but they're not the good kind. *You are freaking out.* You know you are about to marry the wrong man. What's going through your mind?

I was standing at the end of the aisle thinking, "Shit, when am I going to get divorced?"

I kept listening for the music—and the ushers never opened the door. I finally pushed it open myself, like it was a grand performance. I walked down the aisle looking at all of my friends and family whom I did not want to disappoint. At the reception I thought, "Oh my God, what have I done?" I realized I had no emotional attachment to this man.

I was avoiding my dad's eyes as I waited with him at the end of the aisle. I did not want to hear any "pearls of wisdom." Instead

I paid attention to the photographer. I simply could not look at my dad because I knew I was making a mistake.

I was scared to death. I wanted to turn around and run—it felt so surreal, like it was something I was watching and not a part of.

I barely remember the wedding ceremony; it was very simple and it was not special. We didn't even have a honeymoon. I did what I thought I deserved to do at the time. I was totally settling.

I was positively numb and felt like I was in the school play. It was surreal.

As I walked down the aisle, I thought, "Why am I here?" I felt I was too young to get married. (I wasn't—I was twenty-six!) I also told myself that I was never going to have sex with another man again, our sex life was terrible, and our relationship was terrible. . . . Why am I here?

I felt like I was dying a thousand deaths. I just wanted to get the whole thing over with.

And so we begin with what's often the best-kept secret at the wedding: that the bride *knew her marriage was a mistake as she was walking down the aisle.* Whether in a little chapel, a synagogue, or a glorious cathedral—she already knew her marriage was not going to work. In most cases, we're not talking about spur-of-the-moment, Las Vegas weddings. We're talking about marriages that occur after an often lengthy period of dating and engagement.

These quotes are the actual thoughts of brides who knew they were marrying the wrong guys. We asked them to share what was going through their minds in the moments before their wedding ceremonies began. Not the loving, dream-come-true visions of a beautiful wedding day, are they? Imagine having to put on a happy face and feign unbridled joy—with all eyes on you. What's worse is that the majority of the guests are friends and relatives who have known you for years, if not your whole life. You have to put on the performance of a lifetime to fool these people. And, of course, everyone else has expectations of how the bride should appear on the "happiest day of her life."

In all of the pictures, I was walking ahead of him—not side by side. I spent all my time talking to my cousins and hanging out with my gay friend, the pianist.

For those who believed (actually *convinced themselves*) that marriage was what they really wanted, the reality of the day did not match their dreams—as misguided as they were. Their wedding days turned out much differently from the way they had always imagined.

I hated the best man at our wedding. At our rehearsal dinner, I overheard my future mother-in-law in the corner talking to the best man, trying to get him to stop the wedding. She said, "You must stop this! He is making the biggest mistake of his life!" When I told my soon-to-be husband, he said, "Just ignore her."

My wedding day was one of the worst days of my life. My groom got bombed, completely shit-faced. At one point he kicked a chair out from under someone and screamed "FUCK YOU!" at one of the guests. Of course, I had to take care of it.

And the worst part of all? It was too late to turn back. While their insides told them to run away, their outsides kept marching down the aisle. Unfortunately, too many women get so caught up with the idea of being "in love" or "being married" that they forget about the most important part—the relationship itself.

The Worst-Kept Secret at the Wedding

And sometimes it's *not* just the bride who knows the marriage is a mistake. Her friends, family, and the wedding party know it's all wrong, too. It's like watching a car go over a cliff. Think about it: Have you ever been to a wedding and placed a silent bet that the marriage wouldn't last? And it doesn't have to be anything dramatic. Both the bride and groom can be wonderful people—they're just not wonderful for each other.

There was a lot of crying at my wedding. Myself, my friends, my dad. None of us said that it was because of a looming mistake, but it was crying for loss, not for joy.

Many of the women you will meet in this book shared a secret: *I know I am marrying the wrong guy.* But instead of facing their fears in the early stages of their relationships (the fear of being alone, of letting their families down, of being labeled a "failure," of not knowing what the future would bring), they all walked down the aisle anyway. They're sharing their stories in the hope that you will avoid the tough lessons that they had to learn. You'll also hear from those who *did* find the courage to call off their weddings, as well as women who have been happily married for many years and understand the importance of marrying the *right* man. They share their insights about what's important to consider when choosing a life partner, and caution that some guys may make great boyfriends, but not-so-great husbands.

Important Things to Keep in Mind as You Read This Book

1. The women we interviewed were of many different ages, races, religious backgrounds, and educational and socioeconomic circumstances. They also come from different parts of the United States. Their stories, however, are remarkably similar. This tells us that these thought patterns, behaviors, and mistakes are universal. So pay attention to them!

2. We believe that every woman knows, deep down, what is right for her. We hope these stories will serve as a wake-up call to help you recognize your own hazardous relationship patterns and behaviors.

3. If you think that this book does not apply to you because you are not in a relationship or not yet engaged— please think again. The collective wisdom found in these pages can help you better articulate your vision for your life. What kind of relationship do you want? What are the important characteristics that you desire in a boyfriend or hus-

band? Do you even want to get married? Maybe you don't, and you are really looking for something else.

4. We hope that these stories will trigger you to take action. Every bad boyfriend who gets dumped, every misguided wedding that gets canceled, and every disputed diamond that is returned to the jeweler will be considered a success story!

5. Don't be afraid to mark up this book. Turn back the corners of the pages, underline, highlight, and ask yourself the questions you find in each chapter. This will help you uncover the truth. Let's start with the first set of questions. Please keep them in mind as you move through the book:

- Are you settling for a relationship that does not fulfill you?
- Do you recognize yourself in any of these stories?
- Are you ignoring red flags in your current relationship?
- What is your gut telling you about your current relationship?
- Are your cold feet trying to tell you something?
- Do you want to end your relationship but are afraid to be alone?
- Are you trying to talk yourself *out* of canceling your wedding (even though you know you should)?
- Do you want to get married? If so, why?
- What kind of vision do you have for your married life?

Ultimately, the answers and the solutions lie within *you*. This book will help you find them.

Why Are All the Quotes Anonymous?

✦

*Y*ou may have noticed—or will soon—that there are no names attached to the quotes in this book. This was a difficult decision for us to make. The women we spoke with are quite real, and their stories are here in their own words . . . so why not provide even first names?

First and most important, almost all of the women requested anonymity. They agreed to be interviewed, to fill out questionnaires, to answer highly personal questions and give honest answers, but they clearly wanted their individual identities to remain private. This subject, for most of them, was not pleasant to remember and talk about, no matter how many years had passed.

So why *did* they talk? For one reason and one reason only: *to help women like you.* To help you recognize the warning signs, to give you the courage to back out of a relationship or an engagement that would result in a disastrous marriage. To save you from the heartache they went through.

We did consider attaching pseudonyms to each quote, but they turned out to be cumbersome and distracting. The women are real. Their stories are real. We respect their privacy and thank them for letting you hear their stories. We think that after reading this book, you will, too.

✦

PART I

How
Not to Date
the Wrong Guy

✦ 1 ✦

Searching for Happily Ever After
The Top Five Reasons Women
Date the Wrong Guys

No man is worth your tears, but once you find
one that is, he won't make you cry.

—Author unknown

How Not to Date the Wrong Guy

How do you marry the right guy? For starters, don't keep dating the wrong one! After reflecting on their mistakes, hundreds of women we talked to realized their troubles began when they settled for less-than-fulfilling relationships. They knew they weren't right— yet they stayed. They plodded along, ignoring their gut feelings and the obvious red flags. They fell into a rut. They invested time with men who were not right for them. In other cases, it was just a matter of timing. A woman would say, "It's time for me to get married," and she would decide to turn her next date or boyfriend into "the one." But he was not "the one," and deep down she knew it. She ignored her inner voice, and the next thing she knew, she was standing at the end of the aisle wondering, "How did I get here?"

Are You Dating the Wrong Guy?

A woman of any age can date the wrong guy. The unhealthy patterns start as early as freshman year in high school. In fact, we'll go out on a limb and say there are plenty of middle school girls out there who are putting up with things from boys that they shouldn't. We talked to fifteen-year-old girls and fifty-year-old women and heard the exact same things. They know he is wrong, yet they remain in the relationship.

There are many reasons why we shut out that little voice that is trying to warn us that something is amiss. We asked dozens of women of all ages: Why did you remain in an unhealthy relationship or settle for someone with whom you were not genuinely compatible? When we evaluated their responses, universal themes and patterns emerged:

- Loneliness and insecurity
- Belief that a relationship is a solution to problems
- External pressures
- Belief that he will fix her / she will fix him
- Ignore red flags and gut feelings

We'll examine each theme in detail in the pages that follow. But first, see if you can identify yourself in the voices of the women below.

Loneliness and insecurity
I wanted the approval of an older man.

I had feelings of unworthiness. My relationship made me feel better about myself.

He exuded characteristics I did not have. He was confident and cool.

I stayed with the relationship because of my own insecurities and because of emotional abuse. He also made me feel like I couldn't make it on my own. My ex would give me just enough emotion for me to want more; therefore, the emotional abuse cycle was not broken.

He made me feel really loved. He was very charismatic.

I stayed with him because of the same old insecurities; I think I have a strong need to be loved and to love.

I was needy and lacked self-confidence, despite my professional success. I sought to fill that gap with a man.

I thought I was lucky to be with him—that I could learn a lot from him.

In my family, I saw that success meant attracting a lot of men. I sort of did that—I got a man because I couldn't support myself without one.

I think it was partial desperation—I wanted to love someone, and I wanted someone to love me.

It took some time to realize it was wrong, and most of the time I told myself it was OK, just so I could have the comfort of a relationship and having someone in my life.

Belief that a relationship is a solution to problems
I did not want to keep floundering in my life all by myself.

I was not that happy with my day-to-day life. Six of my good friends from college were married already, and I wanted to be married, too. When I met him, I immediately set my sights on him and decided he was good marriage material. That was it.

I wasn't very happy in my professional life. I didn't like my job and was unclear about what to do next. I was sort of in a rut. I think that is why I was susceptible to a poorly-thought-out relationship.

External pressures
My age (twenty-eight) was creeping up on me, and I was not dating much—so I was attracted to him.

I stayed because of peer pressure. I was going to break up with him, but my friends decided that it hadn't been long enough for me to really gauge whether I liked him.

All of my friends were dating seriously or getting married, and I thought that I should be in a serious relationship, too. I think I subconsciously planned on getting serious with the next person who came along. It didn't really matter who it was.

Belief that he will fix her/she will fix him

He was really aggressive and had anger issues, but I, being the person that I am, thought that I could fix that.

I felt maternal instincts for him. "I can fix you—I can be your hero, your savior."

I had delusions it would all work out.

I convinced myself I could make any relationship work. I would be whoever I needed to be to make it work.

I always have this relentless faith that he will change for me or that everything will work out if we keep trying.

Ignore red flags and gut feelings

I was in love with the idea of the boy I dated in high school long before I really got to know him. He was smart, good-looking, funny, a star athlete, and from a good Catholic family. And my parents and friends loved the idea of us together as well. I don't think he was concerned with making me happy; he was too concerned with his own happiness. He complained when things did not go his way, and it brought me down. I was too concerned with his happiness, too, because I had him on a pedestal before I knew him.

Honestly, I always had a gut feeling he wasn't the right one, even from our first date, but I went with it because he really pursued me. This was my first long-term boyfriend, and I thought that I

*just had to put up with things that he did. In fact, I tried to
break up with him after one and a half years because he cussed
at me every day.*

*He made me feel so special and loved. Despite him cheating on
me every time we were together, I felt like it didn't matter. I convinced myself he loved me more than those other girls he hooked
up with.*

Why Do We Date?

What is the purpose of dating? Obviously, it's a social thing.
Men and women are drawn to one another; they want to
spend time together. At school, in bars, at the office, or online, single men and women seek out the companionship of
the opposite sex. It is part of being human—the perpetua-
tion of our species. Men and women hook up, pair off, and
connect every day. But dating also serves another purpose. It
helps us figure out what we want and what we *don't* want in
a long-term partner. As one woman told us:

*I think you can learn a lot from dating the "wrong" guys.
Whether it's a bad experience or just someone who you may not
be completely compatible with, there's usually a lesson in the situation that you can take to your next relationship, in a positive
way.*

Friendships work the same way. We learn about other cul-
tures and religions. We discover new ways of doing things. We
observe different ways of relating to one another. We see

things we want to emulate and things we want to avoid at all costs. One woman said that dating is like "trying on a new personality." It allows you to experience the world in new ways.

Unfortunately, not all women are strong enough to get out of a relationship after they recognize it's wrong. They try on a new personality (usually it's their boyfriend's personality) and the next thing they know, they are living someone else's life.

I wasn't much of an outdoorswoman. Sure, I had been a Girl Scout and gone camping with my family a few times, but that was it. I started dating a guy in college who was a total mountaineer—like Bear Grylls! He hiked, he kayaked, he rappelled, and he loved to camp. It was all he thought about. He was a super-nice guy, so I went along with it and started spending practically every weekend in the woods. I completely took on a new identity as super-outdoor-nature girl—even though I wasn't really thrilled with it. It was hard to break things off, because there were so many things that I did like about him. I had never envisioned my life this way. Well, one thing led to another, and the next thing I knew we were married and living out in the middle of nowhere on a fire station. It was crazy. I was living his dream—not mine.

That's kind of an extreme example, but it's what can happen if you date the wrong guy. You must be honest about whether the relationship is right for *both* of you.

When I know the relationship isn't going to work—I end it. There is no reason to stay with someone when you know it's not going anywhere. I would rather be out trying to find the next one who could be Mr. Right.

That's a fact. You'll miss out on the chance to meet the right guy if you're settling for the wrong one.

✦   ✦   ✦   ✦

Dating in the Age of MySpace, Facebook, Twitter, and Texting

Ask anyone who dated *before* the advent of Facebook and texting, and they will usually say, "I am so glad that wasn't around when I was younger!" The consensus is that it confounds an already complicated process. If the agony of waiting for a returned call is not bad enough, you now have twenty-four-hour access to a guy's Facebook or MySpace page. We asked three young women to weigh in on the pros and cons of dating in the age of Facebook.

For this woman, technology revealed her boyfriend's jealous streak and her own lack of trust:

Facebook and texting were actually the main complications in my relationship. I was in a two-year relationship that just ended recently because of technology like this. Guys would text me while I would be with my boyfriend, and he would get very upset. Or when he wasn't in the room I would look through his phone and see things he would be texting that I wouldn't like. It's so easy to be sneaky on Facebook with the private messages and texts that can be deleted and virtually not exist. It's a really sad situation.

This woman says the constant communication stresses her out:

I think all of the technology just makes everything more stressful. Seeing every person your boyfriend comes in contact with on Facebook just causes too much worry. And sometimes constant texting and communication causes the initial flame to die out faster.

Another woman believes technology is a good thing:

I think technology helps. It's good to see what people are like when they are not trying to put on a show for a good first impression.

In the movie *He's Just Not That into You,* Drew Barrymore's office-mate warns her that "MySpace is the new booty call." It's true. It's another way that guys can reach out to you and mess with your head. And you shouldn't come running every time a guy posts a comment on your MySpace page. You have to be cautious. You also have to pay attention to the clues revealed by someone's texting and status updates. They can reveal red flags. Here are some things to keep in mind when using the various forms of twenty-first-century communication:

Facebook Upside

Facebook can catch a liar and eliminate a lot of excuses. If he says, "Sorry I didn't call. I was out of town," you'll know it's not true because you've been monitoring his status updates ten times a day.

Facebook Downside
You can easily turn into a cyberstalker—don't monitor someone's Facebook status ten times a day! It is unhealthy.

Instant Message Upside
He'll make his feelings clear if you are both online and he never sends you an IM.

Instant Message Downside
You can spend hours online testing him to see if he sends you an IM.

Text Message Upside
He'll show you whether he will tolerate your friendships with other men by monitoring your incoming texts. It is all about trust.

Text Message Downside
Trust works both ways. Don't snoop on his incoming texts. If you don't trust him—that's a red flag!

Cell Phone Upside
There is no excuse for a communication blackout. If he doesn't call, he's telling you he is not interested. That is valuable information.

Cell Phone Downside
It's never a good idea to obsessively wait for the phone to ring.

Cell Phone Upside

If a guy does call you and talk, it's a sign that he likes you and enjoys having a real conversation.

Cell Phone Downside

Beware the guy who only texts you and never calls.

The bottom line is this: Use caution. Don't get obsessed. Pay attention to how a guy treats you. Social networking sites, cell phones, and the Internet are all good ways to gain further insight and clues about a guy. However, as in all areas of your life, use these tools in moderation.

✦

Saying Yes to a Second Date, but No to a Third

Most young women said they would give a guy a chance for a second date—even if things seemed a little "off" on the first. Why?

I wanted to give him a second chance and see if maybe my first impression was wrong.

I thought things would go better than the first date.

Everyone deserves a second chance. Plus, not everyone is good at first impressions, so I think it's OK to give a guy one more try. Neither party is as nervous on the second date, so then you can really decide if he's not right for you or if he was just nervous.

Even though I was pretty sure he wasn't the one, I thought a second chance would be good to completely confirm my thoughts . . . and a nice dinner isn't bad, either!

First impressions *can* be wrong. This college senior had doubts after the first date—yet she said yes to a second one:

I'm not entirely sure why I said yes. I knew he was popular and a lot of my friends thought he was cute, so I said I would go out with him again, even though I knew my mom would not approve.

It's nice to give someone a second chance. However, when something doesn't feel right and you say yes to a third date, you better proceed with caution. That's where you'll get into trouble. Ask yourself: Why am I agreeing to go out with a guy who I know, deep down, is not right for me? Go back to the beginning of the chapter and review the five reasons women stay in relationships that are wrong for them. Otherwise, you may fall into the same trap! One savvy twenty-year-old said, "Sometimes you don't want to believe the obvious (or they don't) and a second date finds its way into your schedule." She's right. But when that second date turns into a third and a fourth . . . you'll suddenly find yourself dating the wrong guy.

Red Flags Trigger Gut Feelings

Unfortunately, far too many women stick around long after they know a relationship is not going anywhere. They tolerate all sorts of unhealthy, unhappy, energy-depleting behavior from their boyfriends. We call these red flags. Red flags trigger your gut feelings. That's the little voice in your head, the funny feeling in the pit of your stomach, or the sense that something is just not right. We'll explore these in depth later, but we wanted to introduce you to them now because they should be on the top of your mind whenever you go on a date. Train yourself to pay attention to them. We asked college girls and twenty-somethings to tell us about the red flags they observed in their former boyfriends.

When he wasn't around me, he was super-cocky to his friends, and when they told me about that I never believed them. I couldn't imagine the guy that I dated to be like that. I guess he always thought of himself as better than everyone else, but I didn't realize how bad it was until I was out of the relationship. He also had a weird relationship with his parents that I didn't like. They would scream and fight a lot, and he was condescending to his mother and younger brother. Around Christmastime, we were getting ready to exchange gifts and he opened his first and he was like, "Oh, well, I guess I expected this because I always out-gift you anyway." I had bought him three DVDs, tickets to a professional baseball game, and made him a card that I spent days working on.

I always felt like he was never being completely honest, avoiding topics that were important to me. Basically, he exhibited sketchy behavior.

He always told little white lies. He didn't appear to lie about anything major, but the white lies made me question his in-

tegrity and whether he was truly invested in our relationship. (He wasn't!)

He still talked to his ex all of the time. I also found out that he had been lying to me. He was really cheap and never wanted to take me out for dinner or anything. We just hung out all of the time. He also wanted to keep our relationship a secret from our friends, which should have been a big red flag.

He would overreact easily and say really mean and hurtful things. Later, he would try to take them back and say he didn't mean it.

He was clingy and overprotective.

All of these red flags triggered gut feelings in these women. They didn't like how their boyfriends behaved, yet they stuck with them longer than they should have. The key is not just recognizing what you are feeling but also finding the courage to do something about it. That may mean talking about your concerns, saying no to another date, or ending the relationship altogether. The goal is to take action. Otherwise, you'll find yourself on a slippery slope, falling into a dead-end relationship.

Listening to That Little Voice in Your Head

We asked women to describe their gut feelings about their pending marriages. What was that little voice inside of them trying to say?

Someone called my parents' house and said, "Whatever you do, do not let your daughter marry him!" When that happened, I knew that I had to call it off. My little voice said, "Someone is looking out for you and it is not your fiancé."

My voice inside my head kept telling me, "You know this is wrong. You are not marrying him because you love him and can't imagine your life without him. You are marrying him because you don't want to be alone anymore and you are tired of the dating scene." Also, I knew that part of what appealed to me was that my fiancé was quite wealthy, and we would lead a very nice life if we married. I knew that I had a lot of self-confidence issues and that I had chosen to be engaged from fear of loneliness. I had agreed to the engagement because I didn't love myself enough, not because I loved him. So my little voice was saying, "Don't use marriage to hide from what you know you need to work on about yourself."

I had a nightmare the first night we slept in our new house. I found myself searching for someone who represented true love. Realizing that I might never feel true love again scared the hell out of me. The little voice inside my head said that I needed to take some time to myself to sort things out. I asked my fiancé the next day if he would give me some alone time in our house, that I really needed it to gather my thoughts. He left for a measly forty-five minutes! When I asked him why he had come home so soon, his response was, "Where am I supposed to go?" That was a huge sign to me that I would be smothered by this man the rest of my life. I literally couldn't breathe.

✦   ✦   ✦   ✦

Red Flags Versus Deal Breakers

It's important to make the distinction between red flags and deal breakers. Red flags are actions, attitudes, and behaviors that make you uncomfortable. Deal breakers are things that should make you end your relationship immediately. Some examples of deal breakers are infidelity, physical or emotional abuse, and active drug addiction. Until these issues are addressed, you are in danger. Make sure you know what your deal breakers are, and never make excuses to justify them!

✦

Dating Lessons Learned the Hard Way

It's easy to find yourself dating the wrong guy. It doesn't matter how old you are, where you live, your educational level, or your career. Smart women make the same mistakes when it comes to men. So what do the young women we interviewed want to tell you about dating? They share their hard-earned wisdom in their own words:

Examine your motives. Why do you think you want something? I've learned that rationalizing is very powerful and you are probably talking yourself into settling for less than you deserve.

Don't try to date someone because you are right for them. They need to be right for you! You are worth it! Don't try to fix anyone or change anything about who you're dating. The right guy is out there. Just make sure you give him a chance. At the same time, don't waste your time on someone who's not right for you. Trust your gut! If you know in your heart that he's not the one for you, have the courage and respect for yourself to break up with him and start looking again.

Don't stay with someone just because it is a habit. Eventually there will be nothing there for you, and you will be stuck. Get out when you realize that you need someone else—someone who will treat you better. It is better for both of you!

If something just isn't clicking with a guy, don't try to hold on to him hoping you can change him into what you want. You can't change a guy; he has to want to change for you. I also believe that everyone deserves a second chance in a relationship. Remember that saying "Fool me once, shame on you. Fool me twice . . . shame on me."

If there are any doubts about his personality, get out, because his flaws are only going to get worse. Physical habits might be changeable but his personality is hard-wired, and nothing is going to change him.

A red flag is a red flag. Get out, and don't stay in the relationship hoping it will get better or he'll change. You deserve better than that and owe it to yourself. Start finding yourself the right man instead of wasting your time with the wrong one who you want to be the right man. Also, if your friends don't approve, there has to be a reason. Don't just blow it off because you think your relationship is perfect. They aren't jealous; they are trying to help.

If somebody doesn't give you the time of day, move on. Most college-aged men are not looking to date a girl long-term. If they do start a relationship with you and it works, that's great. But don't plan for that to happen. Also, it is wonderful when a twenty-year-old-guy treats you well, but keep in mind that you shouldn't treat him like dirt. Most girls I know get upset when they get burned, but forget how many times they have done it to guys! Be nice, be funny, have your own life, and keep an eye out for a nice, respectable man. And don't date a gay guy. (Authors' note: Wonder if she learned this the hard way?)

We couldn't agree more! When it comes to not dating the wrong guy it is quite simple: Think about what you really want in a relationship and never settle for anything less. It's not about being picky. It's about truly defining what you want in your life and respecting yourself enough to not waiver.

Think about it this way. A new restaurant opens up in your city. Everyone is talking about it, and you can't wait to give it a try. When you finally get a reservation, your expectations are high. You arrive and the place is oozing with ambiance. It's packed with the who's who of your city. When your waiter finally shows up, he has an attitude. He rattles off the dinner specials with a detached air of boredom. "That's OK," you think. "He's just busy." You place your order excitedly and wait . . . and wait . . . and wait. An hour goes by before you lay eyes on your salad. The service is subpar and so is the food. It's a new restaurant, though, so you give it the benefit of the doubt. When your steak arrives it's cold and overdone. Disappointment starts to creep in. "I really want to love this place," you think. "Everyone says it's so great!" You order dessert and the waiter informs you that they have run out of the tiramisu you had your heart set on. What a letdown! The whole night has turned out wrong.

What are the chances that you would ever set foot in that restaurant again? Probably pretty slim. You wanted to be treated like a special guest. You wanted a steak that would satisfy your taste buds like never before. You wanted to end your meal with a sinfully sweet dessert that made you cry out for more. You will do whatever it takes to find a restaurant that satisfies all of those qualities. And if they don't give you what you want, you won't return. So why don't you set those same high standards and expectations when it comes to your relationships? Give the restaurant a second chance. Go on a second date. But if you get the same cold steak and surly attitude, have the sense to call it quits.

What Can You Do to Make Sure You Are Not Dating the Wrong Guy?

1. Think about the reasons that you said yes to a second date with a guy who did not make a great impression on you. Did you say yes to a third or fourth date? Why or why not?

2. Think about red flags you have observed in former or current boyfriends. What were they?

3. Think about your deal breakers. Have you ever continued to date a guy even though you knew there was a serious problem, such as emotional abuse or active addiction?

Can You Do to Make Sure You Date the Right Guy?

1. Think about some previous relationships that didn't work out. Did you stay for any of the following reasons?

- Did you feel lonely and insecure?
- Did you think the relationship could solve your problems?
- Did you feel external pressures to stay in the relationship?
- Did you think he would fix you / you would fix him?
- Did you ignore red flags and gut feelings?

2. Were there other reasons? What were they?

3. Hold on to what is important to you. Don't change your personality. Don't lower your standards. Be conscious of what you want and what your values are.

4. It is important to know what a healthy relationship looks like. After fifteen years of working with couples, and countless hours of research, we have observed the following characteristics in healthy relationships. How many of these qualities can you find in your current relationship?

- You bring out the best in each other, not the worst.
- You trust each other; each can count on the other to do the right thing.
- You both appreciate each other's authenticity and allow each other to be autonomous.
- You appreciate all the parts that make your partner whole without needing him to change, or vice versa.

- You do thoughtful things for each other without asking for anything in return (or keeping score!).
- You have fun together.
- You genuinely miss each other when you are apart.
- You share common core beliefs and values.
- Sexual intimacy may not always be a roaring fire, but when it dies down, the glowing embers are easily stoked!
- If you have children, you take the time to attend to each other as a couple and not just as parents.
- You communicate with each other out of care and concern instead of judgment and criticism.

Even if you don't have all of these characteristics in your relationship, deep down you know if it is working or not. Your gut knows. This list should serve as a guideline for what you seek (or what you know needs fixing) in your own relationship.

✦ 2 ✦

Relationship Warning Signs
Red Flags and Gut Feelings

Caution is the eldest child of wisdom.

—Victor Hugo

What Are Red Flags?

One way to practically guarantee an unhealthy, unhappy relationship is to ignore the red flags a guy exhibits while you are dating. What are red flags? The term comes from the use of red flags in real life. A red flag or red light on a railroad means to stop immediately. Red flags are flown to alert people of potential danger or peril. A red flag flown by the armed forces indicates live-fire exercises. Red flags on a beach indicate dangerous water conditions; a hurricane warning is two red flags. They are indicators that should make you stop and take notice. Go no further. Pay attention: Danger ahead.

Red flags in relationships are seriously unappealing or problematic actions, attitudes, and behaviors exhibited by your partner. But red flags aren't always so obvious—they are not just "bad" behaviors, such as dishonesty or infidelity. Vastly differing beliefs or likes and dislikes (religion, jobs, parenting style, and so forth) are also red flags. Whatever they are, red flags should make you stop and think. They offer clues about your boyfriend's character. Ignore them at your own peril.

Do You Have Red Flags in Your Relationships?

People offer clues about their character every day—both good and bad. Let's talk about the bad stuff. These red flags provide hints that your courtship or married life will be unhappy. Let's say you are dating someone who has a short fuse. He is quick to anger and easily irritated. He is argumentative and constantly gets into heated discussions with the store clerk, the gas attendant, and the waiter . . . or worse yet, your relatives. This is a big red flag. What kind of a father do you think this man would be? Children can test anyone's patience. How do you think he would handle a dinner table filled with noisy toddlers? What kind of employee would he be? Would he have difficulty holding on to a job or getting along with his colleagues? Is your future social life already in jeopardy because no one will want to invite "Mr. Volatility" to their parties?

We asked our brides to tell us about the red flags they observed (and subsequently ignored) in their boyfriends. These common themes arose:

- Avoidance
- Dependence
- Extreme differences
- Irresponsibility

- Family issues
- Meanness

Red Flag: Avoidance

Your boyfriend avoids your questions, your company, and conversations about your relationship.

The red flag for me was that he never wanted to make decisions regarding the marriage. His responses were always, "I am really stressed out because of work right now. Can we talk about it later?" At first this didn't bother me because he did, in fact, have a very stressful job. However, even when he seemed relaxed, as soon as the word "marriage" came up, he was suddenly stressed out from work again and became defensive and argumentative. Work was his cure-all excuse.

He ignored me. He would listen to the radio, watch TV, and read the newspaper all at the same time.

He would stand me up or be four hours late for dates—with no apologies or explanation.

If your boyfriend chooses to spend most of his time with his friends instead of spending time with you, this can become problematic as well. What is so much more appealing to him about those friends? Does your partner socialize often with his coworkers? Have you been introduced to them? Why or why not? Are they even aware that you exist? (One woman we'll hear from later discovered that her new husband had never even mentioned to his coworkers that he was engaged or had a fiancée. They were shocked to see the wedding announcement in the local paper!) You don't need to be joined at the hip, but being able to share outside friendships is important. And he should *want* to share you with the folks he spends time with.

Red Flag: Dependence

Does your boyfriend have any friends?

I was his only friend. His dependence on me alone was exhausting. It was very stressful to be his only friend.

He was not even employed when we met. He held a grudge against my parents for kicking me out of their home, but I had already forgiven them and moved on. When we argued he would take my keys or pull the spark plugs from the car so I would not leave. I was a very social person and he was not. He would get angry that I wanted to go out with my friends. He would make me feel so guilty about wanting to spend time with them, instead of him.

What does it mean if your boyfriend doesn't have any friends? One of our brides told us how challenging it was to be married to a man who had virtually no friends:

He was solely dependent on me. He never went "out with the guys" because most of his friends were female. He had no life of his own. He was such an introvert, and he always resisted going to family parties.

"Birds of a feather flock together." "You can judge a man by the company he keeps." You may have heard these sayings from your parents or teachers somewhere along the line.

Does an honest man hang out with a bunch of thieves?
an honorable man enjoy the company of cheaters? Not
cording to this now-divorced woman:

*He didn't have many friends; in fact, his best friend was a
bookie. Later on, I realized he was a compulsive gambler.*

This shouldn't have come as a big surprise.

Father Pat Connor is a Catholic priest in New Jersey. He
has been giving the same lecture to high school girls for more
than forty years. The topic: "Whom Not to Marry." One of
his key tidbits of advice is to *never marry a man who has no
friends.* This is an easy one to figure out. Either he has friends
or he doesn't. Are his friends good guys or not?

Red Flag: Extreme Differences
**You and your boyfriend have differences that cause
problems.**

*I am a very outgoing person. My family always joked with me
when I was little and said I could make friends with anyone. I
almost always have a smile on my face, I have an optimistic attitude, and I am independent. My fiancé, on the other hand,
was not at all like me. He was very reserved and shy, never
cracked a smile, and just in general never seemed like he was
happy. Friends of mine even called him the mortuary worker
after we broke up because he was so stone-faced all of the time.*

*He had a "poor" mentality. He never wanted to eat out. He ate
very simply: cans of tuna, right out of the can. (He could have
afforded to eat out if he wanted to.)*

They say that opposites attract; *polar* opposites, however, have their work cut out for them. There are many instances where major differences are too difficult to overcome. We'll examine socioeconomic differences as an example.

When Julia Roberts and Richard Gere drove off into the sunset in their limousine in *Pretty Woman,* it seemed like the perfect happily ever after. She had achieved the dream of becoming Cinderella, but let's be real. She may have learned the proper etiquette of living an affluent lifestyle, but how would her prince have fared at *her* family's holiday meal?

You can see it now. He shows up in his Armani suit while the rest of the men have on their favorite '80s rock-band T-shirts, which also serve as napkins that catch the grease from their fried chicken dinner. He's not sure where to park his shiny silver Lexus because there are too many pickup trucks and four-wheelers in the way. The real trouble begins when he asks for a "single-malt scotch served neat" and someone offers him a hit off of the beer bong instead.

There are two key issues to consider when it comes to socioeconomic differences. One is money and the other is social class. Let's look at the money issue first. Do you come from a family that is financially successful? Are you used to getting what you want, when you want it? Have you thought about how this will be different when you are married? How will your fiancé feel about going on family vacations that are funded by your parents? Will your lifestyle expectations change, or will you still shop at Saks Fifth Avenue on a Target budget? Conversely, will it be hard to switch from a frugal lifestyle to an affluent one? How you spend money, what you choose *not* to spend money on, and agreement on a budget are all issues that must be explored early in a serious relationship.

Social class differences can be very difficult waters to navigate. Does blue blood flow through his family's veins while your family is blue collar? Is this a source of tension? Does his family reject you because you are not a debutante? On the flip side, does your family look down on him because he didn't grow up at the country club? We understand that there are plenty of incorrigibly rude wealthy people. And a lack of money does not translate into a lack of class—we get that. However, these differences can be a major source of tension. What's most important is that you and your boyfriend acknowledge them and talk about them. Plenty of men and women have married someone from the so-called other side of the tracks and been blissfully happy. The crux of the matter is whether you face this issue head-on—as a team. If his family looks down on you, does *he* support you? Or does he tolerate this treatment of you? Or, on the other hand, if your family is well off, how does he handle it? Does he put them down and call them snobs because they are rich? This is something that must be addressed. You'll learn everything you need to know about his views on money and social class if you observe how he handles these issues while you are dating.

His family had a ton of money. They were nice to me, but I know they would have preferred that he date one of the girls from their blue-blooded circle. The real problem was that while his family had a lot of money, he really didn't. He had a hard time keeping a job. But he spent plenty of time keeping up with his old friends at the country club on his parents' dime. He played golf constantly and drove a Porsche, but it was all for show. I ignored the fact that he didn't have much money of his own. I was kind of blinded by the idea of marrying into this really wealthy family. After we were married, we moved into an apartment because we couldn't afford to buy a house. I tried to talk to him about it, but he didn't get it. He was stuck: a man-child trapped in his privileged upbringing. I got out of there before he dragged my credit down with his. I should have paid attention—he was living this way the whole time we were dating.

Red Flag: Irresponsibility

Your boyfriend can't be counted on (for example, he has a lot of debt).

He was sweet but so irresponsible. He forgot to bring his license to the closing when we bought our house. When he left to go home and get it, he ran out of gas!

Many folks today live in a world of "I want it now." While our grandparents would have never dreamed about charging items they couldn't afford, today's society seems to be digging itself into a financial hole. Financial advisers such as Suze Orman will tell you that not all debt is bad debt. School loans and mortgages are considered good debt and are almost a given during certain seasons of your life. But it's important to take a look at the person you plan on sharing everything with. How much bad debt does he have? Does he have a bunch of "big boy's toys" with monthly payments? A boat or a personal watercraft? A motorcycle? Does he spend more money than he makes? Does he value money? Better yet, will he value the money that *you* bring into the marriage in the same way? Do you need to furnish a new house or apartment? Does one of you need a new car? Are you planning on taking lavish vacations every year? Does he enjoy having expensive material things that do not mean as much to you? Be honest: Is he a ticking financial time bomb that may someday have your name attached to it?

It goes without saying that you must be up-front about *your* financial situation as well so there are no surprises after the honeymoon. The bottom line is this: You *must* talk money and finances before the wedding. The way he handles money now is a good indicator of how he will handle it in the future.

Red Flag: Family Issues
Your boyfriend has a strained—or strange—relationship with his family.

He lived with his mom. She would always pick up after him. Several times I witnessed him stripping naked—totally naked and watching TV. His mom would walk in on him like that. Very strange.

He was an only child, and his mother always made me feel like I was not good enough for her son. His mother and father had divorced when he was young, and his mother hated his father. After my fiancé and I were engaged, she met a man and became engaged, and it was almost like she was keeping up with us. Her ring had to be bigger than mine; her house had to be newer than ours, and so on. It was never like she could just be happy for my fiancé and me; it was like she had to beat us at everything.

You can tell a lot about a person by how he interacts with his family. You must understand that you likely will be treated in a similar manner. A son who really loves his mother and has a healthy relationship with his sisters most likely will have good insight into and respect for other women. There are other men who seemingly have yet to leave the womb. Their mothers *still* run their lives.

I knew he had a weird relationship with his mother, but I kept ignoring it. After we got engaged, all his friends kept asking me what his mother thought. Apparently she was always hanging around his dorm room when he was in college. At our first (of only two) Christmases, the party began at 2 p.m. at his parents' house with a big spread of food and lots of alcohol. Everyone was drunk. When we tried to leave at 4 p.m. to go to my parents' house, his mom was furious. She said, "Where are you going? Why can't she go by herself?" I vowed that this would be the last time I would go to their house for the holidays. My fiancé tried to appease both of us constantly. This should have clued me in. I told him, "Your mother does not love you. She is in love with you!"

Clearly, this umbilical cord was still attached, and it was a lifeline that no other woman could replace. (Fathers, too, can have just as much influence or power in their relationships with their adult children.)

Think about the following family-related issues:

- What are the family traditions that you will be entering into, and are you welcomed there?
- How does your boyfriend speak to his family? Does he speak to them at all?
- How much information about your relationship does he share with his family? Does this include things that only the two of you should be sharing?

Red Flag: Meanness
Your boyfriend is disrespectful and inconsiderate.

He was always belittling me and lying to me. I come from a close family and noticed that his family was not cohesive. They would come for family events, arrive, sit down, eat, and leave. Everyone was just going through the motions. His dad was very belittling—there was underlying sarcasm in everything he said.

He constantly pointed out my shortcomings. The longer we were together, the bolder and more demanding his observations became. Soon, my long hair had to go so that I would look more grown-up. I needed to get rid of my "hippie" clothes and dress more "reasonably." Then he told me that my laugh was too loud, that I opened my mouth too much when I laughed. He told me how to look and behave; nothing I did was adequate. All I wanted to do was please him and make him happy, so I kept buying into his and his family's assessments of my inadequacies.

When we had our first fight he was screaming, "Fuck you!" Even as I left for work, he kept screaming at me. Alarms were going f inside me, but I was madly in love. My maternal instincts kicked in—I empathized and thought I could fix him. He was verbally abusive. He called me terrible, obscene words. I was always walking on eggshells. We had fights; there was turmoil all the time. His family was the same. His mom was always walking on eggshells around his dad. His mom put up with all this crap. He was loaded up with issues.

Does your boyfriend treat you with respect? At the end of the day, you should feel appreciated, cared for, and genuinely loved. Are you spoken to in a way that does not offend you? You are not respected if discussions begin and end with name-calling. Do you feel like you are listened to even when you may agree to disagree? Are you even allowed to disagree with him? It will be virtually impossible to not have disagreements throughout your relationship, so the key is to fight fairly. A respectful partner ends an argument with words like, "I hear what you are saying, but that's not how I feel about it."

Another example of respect is how you are treated in front of others. Are you insulted, put down, or "thrown under the bus" in social situations? If you are allowing this behavior to be acceptable now, it will continue. If you ask him to stop certain actions, or change the way he speaks to you, does he listen? If he does, you are in good shape. If you ask for it to stop and it only gets worse, you are asking for trouble.

✦   ✦   ✦   ✦

A Few Words from Jen on Name-Calling and Profanity

Many women find their way to my couch to talk about problems in their relationships. I admire every person who walks through my door. It takes a great deal of courage to share intimate details of your life with a complete stranger. Over half of my practice involves people who are having serious problems with a significant person in their lives. They show up to talk about their fears, their feelings of abandonment, the pain of things not turning out the way they thought they would. They want another human being to help them understand how they got to that point in the first place.

As the sessions unfold, I am always amazed at how easily many women accept being mistreated. I have spent years researching and understanding cycles of violence in abusive relationships. I know how complicated this type of situation can be. But one thing has struck me over and over: Many women I have spoken to don't blink an eye when their boyfriends/spouses call them names—really awful names, such as bitch, whore, or rag. They think it's normal, acceptable behavior.

I want to set the record straight. It is *never, ever* all right for someone who claims to love you to call you a bitch, or worse. In turn, many of my clients are incredulous when I tell them that my husband has never called me a name in the twenty-two years of our relationship. "Never?" they ask in wide-eyed amazement. *Never!* He will certainly point out when I am acting hormonal, but there is a fine line between telling you that you are acting bitchy and saying you *are* a bitch. It's a very fine line and a dangerous one.

Picture this: You come home late after a long day at work. You were also late picking the kids up from the day care (again) and you now have to pay an extra twenty dollars to the center for your repeated tardiness. You walk in the door, and your husband immediately starts to grill you about why there is no dinner on the table and how you have been wasting your time. The f-bombs start to fly, and both of you become enraged. He calls you a bitch. You take the kids to their rooms and try to escape the feelings of worthlessness that just hit you like a truck. You ask your youngest child to start getting ready for his bath, and your beautiful little boy looks at you and says, "No, bitch!" (Please do not think this is an exaggeration. Children become what they see modeled before them, and this happens more often than you'd think.) You have just set the precedent for not only how you will continue to be treated but how your children will treat others. Is this the kind of life you want for yourself or your future children?

One final thought: How does it feel to be put down day in and day out? Think about a bad boss or a nasty teacher you may have had who criticized, insulted, or made snarky comments about you. You were miserable, right? How will it feel to live with someone who does this to you every day? It won't matter if the world tells you that you're wonderful. All you'll hear are his criticisms ringing in your ears. Don't put up with it.

✦

Major Red Flag: Substance Abuse

Red flags can eventually make your relationship implode. *Major* red flags can blow up your entire life. When it comes to substance abuse and addiction, don't be fooled. You can't fix someone else's addiction. We strongly encourage you to avoid *any* relationship with a man who has an active addiction or substance-abuse problem until he has *at least* one year of sobriety and recovery under his belt. Active participation in an ongoing support or recovery group is also highly recommended.

Your boyfriend uses illegal or prescription drugs or alcohol to excess.
An active alcohol or drug problem is unacceptable in a relationship. We spoke to one woman who knew of her boyfriend's cocaine use but dismissed it as just a casual habit.

When we were dating, I started to realize he was kind of a fuckup. One night before a party he said, "I am going to do coke tonight. If you don't like it you can stay home." He later apologized and I forgave him.

There is nothing casual about snorting coke. If your partner is doing drugs, then he is most likely hanging out with other people who are using drugs. Are these the people that you want to associate with? Think about the financial costs. How much money is being spent on pot, coke, heroin, meth, or even the case or two of beer that comes home every weekend? If you work, do you want your hard-earned money to fund this?

Take a look at how Greg Behrendt and Liz Tuccillo, the authors of the very funny number one *New York Times* best seller *He's Just Not That into You,* respond to a woman who is concerned about her lawyer boyfriend who smokes pot every day:

> Smoking pot makes your brain work slower, and makes you less in tune with your surroundings and more introverted. It dulls your senses and clouds and impairs your sense of reality. So, he's always stoned when he's with you. That really means he likes you more when there's less of you. You're going out with someone that doesn't enjoy you at your full levels. That's tantamount to him liking you better when you're in the other room.*

They offer another bit of advice on alcohol:

> Don't be fooled. Don't let the guy who's not falling down drunk and peeing in his pants get away with the fact that he is quietly, more gracefully, bombed out of his mind every single moment he's with you. It's still inebriation, it's still checking out, and it's still not good enough for you.†

---

*Greg Behrendt and Liz Tuccillo, *He's Just Not That into You: The No-Excuses Truth to Understanding Guys* (New York: Simon Spotlight Entertainment, 2004), 73.
†Ibid.

Major Red Flag: Addiction

Your boyfriend displays signs of other addictions, such as to pornography, gambling, or food.

Addictions can come in various shapes and sizes. Folks will often minimize the seriousness of an addict's behavior because he isn't the stereotypical gutter bum who is picking through garbage and living in a box. Addicts are not just drug users and alcoholics. Addictions to gambling, food, exercising, shopping or spending money, sex, and pornography are becoming common.

One of today's most damaging addictions is to Internet pornography. Gone are the days of husbands hiding their stashes of *Playboy* magazines under the bed. As the Internet continues to stream into our workplaces and homes, the access that people have to pornography can be compared to water. It's flowing directly into your home through the "pipe" that is the World Wide Web. Although it remains a taboo subject, pornography is having a major impact on relationships in this country and around the world.

While researching this book, we went to an online "second thoughts" forum where we saw the pleas for help from a woman who was upset because her fiancé was going to Internet porn sites. She said he logged on *several times a day* and would masturbate. His porn habit was affecting their intimate relationship, and they were having sex only about once a month. He preferred the company of nameless, naked strangers on a computer screen to her. He ignored her pleas to stop. She asked what she should do. Guess what? Most people on the forum took *his* side! They told her, "All guys do this," or "You're being a prude." A few people supported her, but most felt it was normal behavior and wrote that she would just have to "accept it." That is so wrong! Can you say *addiction*? If you are uncomfortable with your fiancé's use of pornography, you do not have to accept it. You are not a prude. All guys do not masturbate in front of their computer screen on a daily basis.

Would you be surprised to find pornography on your boyfriend's computer? How would you feel? How would he respond if you confronted him? That's the most important point of all—would he be willing to stop doing something that makes you unhappy or uncomfortable?

If you are not OK with pornography, if you do not support your boyfriend's drinking and drug habits, if you resent the fact that your boyfriend talks more to his bookie than to you, but you are not prepared to do something about it, here is what you could look forward to:

He was lazy, frequently without a job. And he gambled. It wasn't until after I left him that I found out to what extent.

After I filed for divorce, I found out that we owned a racehorse.

When we were dating he was always a big party boy; but after we got married, I found out that he smoked pot every single day.

Addictions are always destructive, and they come with baggage that goes much deeper than just bad judgment. More often than not, addictive behaviors show up in response to darker, hidden issues. There could be a predisposition to addiction in the family. It could be the brain's chemical response to depression. Or it could be a coping mechanism in response to some sort of trauma, be it physical, sexual, or emotional. What you view as just a carry-on piece of emotional baggage could actually be a U-Haul truck filled to the brim. Good luck trying to unpack it! The good news is that people can lead successful lives and relationships if they get help for their issues. But it is a long road to recovery, and you'd better be prepared to go the distance.

Miscellaneous Red Flags

Here are some others that may trigger your alarm bells:

- Jealousy
- Lying
- Self-centeredness
- Discomfort with intimacy

Your boyfriend is jealous.

He didn't trust me. He could get very jealous, and in my job, I was primarily teaching or working with other men. At first I thought of the jealousy as love. I remember on our wedding night I danced nonstop with my new husband, as well as many cousins and close male friends and family. That night, he revealed to me that he was very angry because I had "ignored" him all night. He never forgave me for this and reminded me of it for the next few years.

My fiancé had been cheated on by past girlfriends, and so he was always questioning my actions. At that point in my life, I was working full-time and going to college in the evenings; I barely had time for myself. Living under a microscope is never fun, and if you do not have trust in a relationship, it is bound to fail.

Your boyfriend is a liar.
He had one fatal flaw that affected everything about our life together: He was a pathological liar. He said he had a college degree and didn't. He lied about a big inheritance, then said his mom stole it. He lied to impress people with his intellect or wealth. He didn't pay bills. He would lie, and then get some kind of thrill over seeing how long he could get away with it.

He was conceited and very full of himself. He also constantly lied. He visited me in college once with hickeys on his neck and told me that I was the only one he was dating. He also hit on girls in front of me all the time. He put his mother and guy friends first, before me. He never complimented me on anything I did.

Your boyfriend is self-centered.
He was materialistic and self-centered. He cared about things, not people.

He called himself "brutally honest," to the point where I would get embarrassed by the things he said in front of other people. He usually came off as arrogant when he explained that he was "brutally honest." He always encouraged me to be confrontational with people and criticized me for finding other ways to resolve conflict.

Your boyfriend is uncomfortable with intimacy.
Every so often when we were having sex, he would sort of force things on me—unexpected things. He would just do it, with no warning.

We did not have a good physical relationship. He always had to watch porn before we had sex.

❖　　❖　　❖　　❖

How to Marry a Dirtbag . . . Literally

- Ignore the fact that he doesn't shower regularly.
- Make excuses for his frequent body odor.
- Look the other way when you realize he doesn't own a toothbrush.

That way, you can't complain about kissing a mouthful of dentures (that you paid for!).

He had poor hygiene. He never brushed his teeth. After we were married he had to get all of his teeth pulled because they were rotten—he had a full set of dentures.

❖

Red Flags Are Different for Everyone

A red flag for you may not be a red flag for your best friend. Let's take a look at what one woman told us about her former fiancé:

He loved to watch televised sports. He would spend ten hours on Saturday and ten hours on Sunday watching back-to-back games on TV. I hated that. I could sit there for about two hours at the most. I don't mind going to a professional football game or baseball game, but it is only fun for me if I am sitting on the sidelines of the actual game, not watching it on the couch. My favorite thing to do on a weekend is to ride my bike, go window shopping, or try out a new restaurant. I like to be busy!

There is no right or wrong here. Everyone has their own likes and dislikes. This is an example of two people with vastly divergent ideas about how they want to spend their free time. The first red flag was that this couple had very different interests.

When I went to visit him (we had a long-distance relationship), I didn't want to sit around and watch TV all weekend. I wanted to explore the city! I wanted to try new restaurants, go see the sites, maybe take in a movie. He would plan maybe one or two things to do on the weekend, but most of our time was spent watching his beloved TV sports. It really bothered me. I didn't complain about it because I wanted the relationship to work out.

The next red flag was that she was starting to change her behavior in response to *his* likes and dislikes. She was giving up the things that she wanted to do in order to maintain peace and keep things moving forward in the relationship.

After a while, I got fed up with sitting around watching games on TV every weekend. I started to complain about it, and he basically said that it was too bad; he wasn't changing. He said he worked hard, had a stressful job, and traveled a lot. This is how he kicked back and relaxed. He had no interest in new restau-

rants, the latest movies, or participating in 5K runs. I thought this was really inconsiderate. But deep down I knew how different we were. I started making plans with some of his friends to do the things I wanted to do around town. I would wake up early and go meet his friends for a run and then we would go out to breakfast, while he was home snoozing. I finally allowed myself to face the fact that this is how my future life with him was going to be. He would sit around all weekend watching TV, and I would be doing things by myself. That might be OK for some women, but it wasn't OK with me.

In the end, neither of them was willing to change. That is OK! The good news is that she recognized the red flags in the relationship and acknowledged them. She knew their differences would lead to problems in the future. She refused to settle for a guy who was content to spend every Saturday and Sunday on the couch.

I lost touch with my ex-fiancé. Hopefully he found a nice woman who kept his beer cold and cheese dip hot all weekend long. I am now happily married to a great guy who loves to do all the same things I do. My husband doesn't even like sports. That's one of the things I love about him!

Red Flags in Your Own Behavior

We also need to talk about *your* feelings and behaviors that may signal trouble. They serve as red flags, too. Are you changing who you are? Have you lowered your standards in order to keep your relationship or planned wedding on track? Do you feel sick or uneasy? What red flags are flying in your own mind? Consider the following questions:

Have you isolated yourself from your friends and family since you met your boyfriend?
Many of the women we spoke to said that as their relationships got more and more serious, they lost connection with their close friends and family members. Some were even encouraged by their boyfriends to do so. A comment such as "You don't need them—you have me now" is an invitation to abandon the people we love and care for. For a few brides, the isolation from family and friends was self-inflicted. They couldn't face them in the midst of their own doubts and shame about their soon-to-be-regretted weddings. This makes perfect sense. If you are lying to everyone you know about a wedding that you are dreading, there's a good chance that you will want to avoid everything and everyone associated with it.

Looking back, I can see some red flags that I should have taken note of. He was rude and disrespectful to his mother and other women in his family. He has no sisters, and his mom was his only female role model growing up. He and his brothers would pick on his mom, and she would allow them to speak to her that way. He often commented on her weight, and how she cooked, cleaned, and treated his father. His dad usually just laughed and encouraged the behavior. Another red flag is that he often disrespected my family members. Not to their faces, but he always talked bad about them to me. Even though he knew how impor-

tant my family was to me, it was like he was trying to turn me against them by always pointing out their negative characteristics and things they did that he did not approve of.

❖   ❖   ❖   ❖

Anne's Story: How Burger King Helped Me See the Red Flags

"Can I order a margarita?" I knew before these words were out of my mouth that I was losing my mind. I was actually asking my fiancé's permission to order a frozen drink. My sister, in town for a visit, about fell out of her chair. She could not believe that her bossy, dominating, and loud big sister was seeking permission for a margarita. Yes, it's true. I had just moved to Chicago to be closer to my fiancé. After just a few weeks of unemployment, job hunting, and subtle put-downs, I was starting to crack up. (And I don't mean laugh.)

I didn't want to move up to Chicago without a job, but due to the high price of airline tickets and the hassle factor of a long-distance relationship, we decided that I would relocate. Not smart. I knew better. (Don't ever quit your old job without securing a new one!) But I told myself I had a nice résumé and impressive job experience. Yet here I was, starting to deteriorate after just a few weeks.

I have heard people wonder why abused women don't "just leave," but it is so much more complicated than that. Earlier that week, I had gone on a 7 a.m. job interview at a radio station. When I was finished, I ran across the street and grabbed an egg-and-cheese bagel from Burger King. I polished off my ninety-nine-cent sandwich and didn't think twice when I threw the Burger King bag in the trash can in his kitchen. Later that night he asked about it. "Well, you sure are spending a lot of money dining out for someone who is unemployed," he told me. Inwardly, I rolled my eyes, but I didn't defend myself to him.

Two days later, I returned for a second interview. Back to Burger King I went for another yummy sandwich. This time, however, I carefully disposed of the evidence before I got home. I realized that this was highly dysfunctional behavior. I was hiding this from him because I knew he would put me down if he saw another Burger King bag. I couldn't believe myself. Just like that, I was starting to walk on eggshells around him.

Later that week, he told me I was using too much toilet paper. *What?* It dawned on me that on a subtle level, I was starting to change. I think it was the combination of unemployment, living in an unfamiliar town, and the realization that I was in the wrong relationship. I felt trapped and weak. My self-esteem was starting to drain out of me like air from a limp balloon. The good news was that my inner self was starting to take control and warn me about the changes in my behavior. I was aware of them. And sometimes that's all you need—awareness. And now, every time I eat an egg-and-cheese bagel from Burger King, I feel empowered!

✦

Are you drinking or using prescription or illegal drugs to ease your stress?

Drug and alcohol use is one of the easiest ways you can escape your feelings. The women on *Sex and the City* were masters at resolving their issues over a couple of cosmopolitans.

Unfortunately, your problems will still be there waiting for you after you cure your hangover—not to mention the many mistakes we all make when our judgment is clouded by vodka and cranberry juice.

How well are you sleeping at night? Are you in the habit of taking a few Valium from your mother's medicine cabinet to help you catch some z's? Your body should naturally be able to slow down and rest when you need it to. Not getting enough sleep can make any sane person crazy, but if lack of sleep is a result of paranoia related to your upcoming nuptials, numbing yourself with drugs and alcohol is not the answer. It's also a clue that something is wrong—a red flag.

Are you letting your boyfriend treat you with less respect and consideration than your friends do?
Think about your friends for a minute. It is interesting to note that women will often tolerate poor behavior or boredom in their romantic relationships, yet they are unwilling to do so in their friendships. Does this ring a bell for you? What would you do if a friend did the following?
- Was inconsiderate of your feelings
- Did not honor special occasions such as your birthday with a card or a phone call
- Did not return phone calls
- Lied to you
- Belittled you
- Bored you
- Did not share the same sense of humor
- Spoke disrespectfully to you
- Drank too much

- Refused to see the movies you wanted to see
- Avoided socializing with your family
- Preferred the company of other friends to yours
- Did not make an effort to spend time with you

If a girlfriend treated you poorly, you would eventually drop her. Why would you tolerate this kind of treatment from your boyfriend? It is unfortunate that we set the bar higher for our friendships than for our romantic relationships. Many times we are willing to make excuses or justify bad behavior in our partners just to keep a relationship moving forward. Our standards should remain the same for our friends and our partners. Are you setting the bar lower for your boyfriend? That's a big red flag!

One woman recalled all the red flags that she observed in her relationship with her now ex-husband:

- *He invited me to move in right away—but it was more for practical reasons.*
- *He did not like sex much—he was very negative about it.*
- *He wanted a "mom" around to clean up and cook for him.*
- *He had a terrible temper and lots of rage.*
- *His family was dysfunctional. His mother had been divorced four times. He had two sisters. One sister lived far away and never wanted to come home to visit the family. The other sister was unhappy and cheating on her husband. (This was the sister to whom he was closest.)*
- *He had lots of acquaintances but no real close friends at all.*
- *He jokingly called me "bitch," saying "beeyaatch" even when I asked him to stop.*
- *He would yell at me, and I would yell back.*

Would she choose a girlfriend like this? Would she let another woman treat her this way? Probably not. Oh, and just in case you are wondering what their marriage was like, she said:

He wanted a mom. He was rude, he was a yeller, we never had sex, his family drove me crazy, and we had no social life. It was miserable and we got divorced.

Your Gut Feelings: The Key to Recognizing Red Flags

By now you should understand that a red flag is anything that triggers a response in your gut. It's the little voice in your head, the funny feeling in the pit of your stomach, or the sense that something is just not right. Let's recap what we've learned about red flags:

- Red flags are troubling actions, attitudes, or behaviors exhibited by your boyfriend.
- Red flags are opinions, beliefs, likes, or dislikes that are vastly different from your own.
- Red flags are different for everyone.
- Red flags can also be changes in *your* behavior in response to your boyfriend.

Think about how your gut reacts to these red flags. You will know what *your* red flags are based on your "gut reaction." Does something make you feel sick to your stomach? Stressed out? Does it just not "sit right" with you?

The more awareness you have of these feelings, the better you can train yourself to pay attention to them. We asked women who almost married the wrong guys to describe their gut feelings in their own words. Did their inner wisdom have a voice? Or was it a physical sensation? A knot in the stomach? Butterflies? Headaches?

I definitely experienced more physical signs, such as anxiety, panic, nausea, and deep depression. It's like these symptoms were under the surface while I was dating him and then when we moved in together, they exploded.

I would definitely describe my instinct as a sick feeling in the pit of my stomach, that sinking feeling you get when you know you have done something wrong. Like when you were a kid and you took something that didn't belong to you—you knew you were wrong because your gut told you so!

This voice physically manifested itself into sleepless nights. I would lie awake at night wondering what to do. Sometimes it was as if I could literally feel my heart breaking.

It was more physical—I wanted to throw up and then I felt fantastic once I called it off!

There was a little of both. I guess right before the bachelorette party, I began distancing myself from him. I was not as physically attracted to him, and it felt like it took all of my effort to be happy with him. I did not want him to kiss me, touch me, or anything; it almost made me nauseous just to think about being intimate.

Leading up to the day we went to see the counselor, I repeatedly had terrible nightmares, in which I was in a natural disaster.

Gut Check

We are all familiar with these sensations. Unfortunately, we tend to ignore them, stuff them, or push them aside. "Do not ignore your gut feelings!" is probably the most important nugget of wisdom you can take away from this book. Every single woman we interviewed admonished herself for ignoring them. Some referred to "the little voice in my head," while others called it "intuition." But no matter what they called it, they all said they ignored it, and that's how they married the wrong guys. Keep in mind that a gut feeling serves as an alarm or internal warning system. When your gut reacts in response to a concern or situation, it means that this system is working properly.

In the central part of the United States, sometimes referred to as "Tornado Alley," many municipalities have tornado sirens evenly spaced along the telephone poles. When a severe storm approaches or a funnel cloud is spotted, the sirens sound a loud warning. It's an eerie sound in the midst of a fierce thunderstorm. When people hear them, they know it's time to take cover or head to the basement. They *react*. In our hometown, the sirens are tested precisely at 11 a.m. on the first Monday of every month. They can be startling, particularly on a bright and sunny day. "What's with the sirens?" we ask, and then we quickly realize it's just a test. It's comforting to know that they are working and ready to go. Well, it's the same with your gut. When it reacts, you know the system is working. The key is whether you are going to pay attention and head to a safe place. Whatever you choose to call these feelings, let there be no doubt that this internal warning system knows what's right for you.

Gut-Buster Checklist

Listen carefully to what that little voice in your head is trying to tell *you* about your significant other. Are there problems in your relationship that you do not want to face? Does your boyfriend exhibit behavior that you *know* spells trouble for your future? Carefully consider your boyfriend's behavior and how he treats you, and let's take a look at some other issues and indicators—all potential red flags—that must be examined before committing to someone.

Red Flags Are *Patterns* of Behavior

✦

*W*e understand that everyone has their bad days. All of us have snapped at a store clerk or gotten testy with a coworker . . . and then regretted it and apologized, we hope. True red flags indicate an *ongoing* pattern of behavior. You don't have to be a psychologist to figure out whether your boyfriend has anger issues or has a problem holding a job. The key is whether you are willing to see these red flags for what they are . . . and for what they mean for your future.

Red Flags + Gut Feelings = *Trouble*

How can you recognize *your* red flags?

• Think about red flags for you. What red flags have you observed in past relationships? What about your current relationship? Write them down and reflect on them.

• Are you changing your behavior in response to your boyfriend or fiancé? Are you isolating yourself, avoiding your friends and family? Do you feel like you are walking on eggshells all the time? Be honest.

How can you connect your red flags to your gut feelings?

• Think about your gut feelings. How would you describe them? Is it a "little voice inside your head"? Is it a "feeling"? What do you call them? Intuition, a sixth sense, your conscience? Be aware of how *you* respond. Make a connection between the red flags and the gut feelings. Here is a sample conversation you might have with that little voice in your head:

RED FLAG: *He is always losing his temper over minor things.*

YOUR GUT FEELING / INTERNAL DIALOGUE: *Every time he yells at the waiter or the pizza delivery guy I feel sick to my stomach. I feel so embarrassed. What if he blows up in front of my friends or family? How will I feel then?*

RED FLAG: *He is constantly telling little lies.*

YOUR GUT FEELING / INTERNAL DIALOGUE: *Every time I catch him in a lie, I wonder what else he is not being honest about. He seems to be dishonest about a lot of things. This concerns me and makes me feel uncomfortable. I don't trust him.*

Regardless of what the red flags are for you, the important clue you need to take away is how *your* gut responds to them. Ignore those feelings and we can practically guarantee you will end up in an unhappy marriage. Learn to recognize them and you are on your way to a happier, more satisfying relationship. The choice is yours!

✦

PART 2

How
Not to Get
Engaged to
the Wrong Guy

◆ 3 ◆

The Race to the Altar
The Top Six Reasons Women Stay in Unhealthy Relationships and Get Engaged to the Wrong Guys

And You Wonder Why It Didn't Last

She married him because he was such a "strong man."

She divorced him because he was such a "dominating male."

He married her because she was so "fragile and cute."

He divorced her because she was so "weak and helpless."

She married him because "he is a good provider."

She divorced him because "all he thinks about is business."

He married her because "she reminds me of my mother."

He divorced her because "she's getting more like her mother every day."

She married him because he was "happy and romantic."

She divorced him because he was "shiftless and fun-loving."

He married her because she was "steady and sensible."
He divorced her because she was "boring and dull."
She married him because he was "the life of the party."
She divorced him because "he's a party boy."

—Author unknown

Heading Down the Aisle with the Wrong Guy

We all make mistakes. We forget to add the baking soda to our cookie dough. We run red lights. We open our mouths and ruin the surprise party. We get distracted or don't pay attention. These are little slip-ups with minor repercussions, and we recognize our mistakes *after* the fact. When it comes to dating, though, we've shown you that a woman will often *know* he's the wrong guy—yet she will stay anyway. We've shared the reasons women date the wrong guys in Part 1. But why do they get engaged to the wrong guys?

It starts when the woman (or sometimes it's her boyfriend) starts pushing for marriage. This raises the question: Why do women push empty or ineffective relationships toward engagement and marriage? Or, why do they allow themselves to be passively "pulled along" and become engaged and get married? In some cases, the women we interviewed had pressured their boyfriends to become engaged. In other cases, they felt pulled along—like it "just happened" to them. Again, those same patterns of insecurity, loneliness, and external pressure emerged. However, three more themes appeared as well. These were financial insecurity, belief that engagement is the next logical step or course of action, and the belief that marriage was the solution to their problems. Again, here is what they told us, organized by theme:

- Loneliness and insecurity
- External pressures
- Financial insecurity
- Belief that engagement is the next logical step or course of action
- Belief that marriage is a solution to problems

Loneliness and insecurity

I think I needed to prove something to the rest of my family. If I got married, it would prove that I was better than them. (Everyone in my family was divorced.)

I thought this would be my one chance to get married; I didn't want to risk letting it go. I was scared to be alone.

I was really still in love with my former boyfriend; he was my best friend and we had lived together. We had a wonderful relationship, but deep down I knew he was gay. We were just like Will and Grace! When I ended that relationship, I immediately fell into another one, even though I was still in love with my old boyfriend. I guess I just didn't want to be alone—that's why I married the wrong man.

I was lonely, scared, and living on loans and grants and fellowships. I was pursuing my graduate degree and had no money, no contacts, and no car. I was from a small town and this was the first time I had been away from home.

External pressures

Half my friends were married, and I wanted to be married, too.

I was twenty-six and that was the age I had always thought I'd get married by and think about starting a family. (Fortunately, we never had kids!)

People were asking me—why aren't you married? I was tired of that question and felt embarrassed by it.

All of my friends were getting married or had serious relationships. It seemed like everyone I knew from high school, college, and work was married or getting married. I guess I felt left out and thought that I had better find someone, too.

I was twenty-eight years old and all my friends were getting married. I think on a subconscious level I decided to make whoever came into my life "the one." Deep down I knew he wasn't "the one," but I stayed with him anyway.

Financial insecurity

I thought marriage would solve my problems; specifically, I would not have to work anymore. I could quit my job.

I saw my fiancé as security—he made good money. I relied on that because I was so miserable at my job.

There was the complicating factor of thinking that this was my only acceptable option in life. I didn't have enough money for college because only wealthy people went to college. This in spite of the fact that I was in the top 10 percent of my graduating class. No one told me about scholarships or the fact that people can work their way through college. I was so oblivious to the options. I hated my father and I couldn't wait to move out of his house, but I had no money to do so, of course. I saw, as my only other option to marriage, continuing to live with my family and work at the local bank. If I got married, I would live in the country and milk cows. Believe it or not, I really enjoyed that. I don't know why I thought I had to get married to do that— I didn't think about just getting a job as a cow herder.

Belief that engagement is the next logical step or course of action

We had dated for a couple of years. Neither of us was getting any younger. I thought I had better marry him so I wouldn't end up alone.

I felt like he didn't want to get married all that much, but we had dated for seven years, and lived together for two years, so I said, "Shouldn't we get married at this point in our extensive courtship?" He agreed, and we got engaged.

We were together for eight years. It was the next step in the relationship. Plus, all my friends were getting married and I didn't want to be an old maid.

Belief that marriage is a solution to problems

While I was happy in my professional life, my personal life was not great. I was grasping for change so I began to focus on my personal life. I thought that if I got married I would be happy, even though I wasn't even dating anyone at the time! I thought that marriage was the solution to my unhappiness.

I didn't feel together in my life; I didn't like my job and had no clear career path. Lots of my friends were getting married and dating very seriously. I thought that I should be doing it, too.

We got engaged at the Four Seasons Hotel . . . I was excited, but in hindsight, I just wanted to be engaged to anyone!

✦   ✦   ✦   ✦

How to Marry a Cheater

- Believe that he is really going out every weeknight at midnight to meet his duck-hunting buddies.
- Ignore your gut feelings about all the time he spends with his secretary.
- Forgive him when he cheats on you before the wedding.

That way, you won't be shocked by an announcement like this:

Eleven months after our wedding we went to his company Christmas party. One of his coworkers pulled me aside and said, "You are a really nice person. . . . I just wanted you to know that he and his secretary are fooling around." That was horrible.

✦

Are You Getting Married for the Wrong Reasons?

Many women believed that marriage would solve their problems—problems in their relationships or problems in their lives. They thought that marriage would change their relationships and make them better. They also thought that being married would make them happier, or more fulfilled. What was really eye-opening is that most women seemed to focus more on the *idea* of marriage or the institution of marriage rather than on *whom* they were marrying.

Here is a scary statistic for you. The authors of *The Most Important Year in a Woman's Life / The Most Important Year in a Man's Life* report that a typical bride will spend 150 to 500 hours preparing for her wedding—the equivalent of one to three months working at a full-time job. However, that same bride will spend only about 15 hours preparing for the actual marriage—the relationship with her husband.*

These numbers should be reversed. More time should be spent evaluating the relationship. Hundreds of hours should be directed toward determining whether the relationship has all the ingredients to withstand the test of time. An engaged couple should spend 150 to 500 hours figuring out how to weather the sickness, not the health, the bad times, not the good, and the poorer, not the richer days of their future marriage. They should also make sure they really want to get married in the first place.

*Susan DeVries, Bobbie Wolgemuth, Robert Wolgemuth, and Mark De-Vries, *The Most Important Year in a Woman's Life: What Every Bride Needs to Know / The Most Important Year in a Man's Life: What Every Groom Needs to Know* (Grand Rapids, Mich.: Zondervan, 2003), 15.

It's important for both partners to have the same goals, beliefs, and ideals driving their decision to wed. If they don't, it's a recipe for unhappiness. Everyone we interviewed had the benefit of hindsight, and they all said the same thing: They got married for all of the wrong reasons.

Under Pressure—I Have to Get Married Now (But I Really Don't Know Why)

Let's take a closer look at the external pressures that push women to get engaged. Almost all of the women we interviewed talked about pressure of one form or another influencing their decisions to marry. They cited unrelenting pressure from their friends, families, and themselves. Others felt that financial pressure or the pressure of passing time led them to accept a diamond ring from Mr. Wrong. Whether it was self-imposed or external, pressure led them to make bad choices.

Family pressure

I started dreading family occasions because my aunts and grand-mas would always give me the third degree about my love life.

I was the oldest cousin in my family that wasn't married. All my cousins were getting married, and I felt like I had to hurry up and get married, too.

I felt that I had to go through with my wedding. I'm from a large family and I was the only surviving daughter. (My sister had passed away in a car accident). My parents wanted a huge party, and a huge party is what they got. My mom and his mom planned the whole thing. All of my friends were getting married, and I wanted to have a wedding with him so bad. I pressured him a lot.

Financial pressure
I was raised in an abusive environment. I was used to being abused and hiding it. I failed myself and did not know how to get out. For some reason I felt that living with this person meant I was supposed to stay. I was not in an economic position to support myself. This was also the first relationship I was really in. I dated in college but was never in a relationship. I was never interested in settling down, and then suddenly I thought that I had no direction in life and being in this relationship gave me something.

I was positively floundering, and I wanted to be settled. So I looked at the man I was dating and thought, this is great! He is older; he is established. (I didn't look close enough, because he was thirty-eight years old and living with his mother!) I didn't want to work and thought that I could stay home and have little brown-eyed, brown-haired babies and make play dates like my sister did!

Pressure of passing time
I was getting older and wanted to be married. He seemed like a nice guy and my family just adored him. I know they wanted me to marry him. I suppose I just didn't think it would turn out years later like it did.

I convinced myself that if I don't do this now, with him, I will never get married. I just wanted to have kids and to be a mom.

Career/lifestyle pressure

At one point during our engagement, my fiancé turned to me and said, "Do you realize if it weren't for the horses, we would not have anything in common?" That should have been a good indicator, but I was not the type to give up on something, and I did truly love him. My line of business is full of travel and is also seasonal, so starting a relationship with someone from the regular working world was hard, if not impossible. Having a relationship with someone in the same business was very attractive and easier to manage. Of course, in our close circle of friends and clients we had a lot in common: polo, horses, and a lot of travel.

Everyone I worked with was married or getting married. If you weren't in a serious relationship, you didn't fit in. They were all doing "couple-type" activities, such as going to the wineries, dinner parties, and weekend getaways. If you weren't part of a couple, you weren't invited.

Pressure to grow up

I wanted to be an adult. I thought by marrying I would become an adult. I didn't know I was already an adult.

Sexual pressure

I felt really guilty because I had had sex with him. I was such a good girl, and I had already gone to bed with him. That really weighed heavily on me. I thought it would assuage my guilt if I married him.

The Problem with Pressure

It's hard to think clearly when we are under pressure. No matter what the situation, we tend to make mistakes when we feel rushed, overwhelmed, and pressured. It's easy to become confused. When you are feeling anxious about your love life, or trying to meet a self-imposed marital deadline, chances are good that you will pick the wrong guy. It becomes a race to the altar. Sound familiar? Don't forget, we are talking *the rest of your life* here. It's vitally important to take a step back and carefully observe what's *really* going on. If you're aware of this pressure and can understand what's pressuring you, you can spare yourself a lot of pain. Proceed with caution.

Reality Check: Why Do You Want to Get Engaged?

We are constantly bombarded with confusing messages about marriage and what it will bring us. If you are single, do you think marriage will bring you instant fulfillment and happiness? Think again! Even a happily married woman will tell you it's not true. Great marriages take work. Furthermore, a happy marriage is the result of two compatible, emotionally healthy, and already-fulfilled people committing to spend their lives together.

Do you want to get engaged because all of your friends are? Are you anxious for your turn to share your adorable how-he-proposed story and flash that fabulous two-karat rock around the office? That's not a good enough reason to get engaged. You need to figure out what you really want and need. We are all ultimately looking for someone to love us. But how do you define love? Think carefully about what your definition of love is. It can't be simply those giddy feelings—butterflies and all that. What you really need is someone who understands you and cares about your well-being. You want to be appreciated and valued. You want to feel cherished and respected.

Don't Be Distracted by the Butterflies!

Be careful and look at the big picture. Make sure that your boyfriend doesn't just *tell* you that he loves you. He needs to *show* you that he loves you, too. Don't be distracted by the butterflies.

My ex really made me feel loved—he was and still is very charismatic. I totally believed in him and gave him everything I had, even though he was drinking too much and having affairs. He was very intense—the best and the worst. It was almost impossible for me to walk away. And like many women, I wondered if anyone else would ever want to marry me.

Guess what? She got engaged to him even though he was drinking too much and cheating on her. And then she married him. Do we really need to tell you how it turned out? Pressure and butterflies can cause intelligent women to make very bad choices.

Anne's Story: My Race to the Altar

◆

It was time for a new job. This became crystal clear as I was struggling to duct-tape Miss Budweiser's breasts. After her breasts were good and smashed, I sprayed her with baby oil to make sure she was sticky, gooey, and glowing for our annual poster. The photographer kept screaming, "Spray her more!"

I know every red-blooded male in America would have switched places with me in a heartbeat. But I was a twenty-eight-year-old heterosexual female who was not particularly enjoying this—even though our photo shoot would take us from a luxury yacht to the beach and back to the yacht club pool. They say that a bad day at the beach is better than a good day at the office. But still, as sweet and friendly as the model was, I didn't enjoy the prep work one bit. I couldn't believe I was doing this. There was not a "sexing and oiling-up poster girls" course in college. It felt wrong. I felt like a traitor to my gender.

As the marketing manager for a beer distributor, I was constantly going from special event to committee meeting to bar promotion. I enjoyed many of the perks, and I loved the people I met.

But after years of night promotions, special events, and long weekends, I was done. I wanted a new job. I was lonely. I was burned out. Many of my friends had responsible careers and were starting to settle down and get married. Kathleen and Patti were teachers. My friend Barb

entist, and Mel and Peggy were making a killing
their sales careers. And I was riding around in a beer
truck and judging bikini contests in bars. I decided it was
time to grow up and be responsible, too.

But I was responsible—I just didn't see it that way. I
had my own apartment. I paid my bills on time. I had car
insurance, life insurance, and health insurance. I even
sent out Christmas cards. But I was traveling up and
down U.S. 1 in southern Florida going to bars every
night. And I—like so many other women—believed that
being grown up and responsible meant being married. So
I decided I better get married. And that's when my future
fiancé walked into our office.

Now, I must qualify this a bit and say that my decision to grow up and marry was not completely conscious. I
didn't totally connect the dots. But my subconscious observations certainly drove my decision. I'm not sure why I
overlooked the complete lack of chemistry and red flags.
But while researching this book, I read something that
made sense and gave me some insight into why I pursued
a relationship with a guy who was all wrong for me.

In Judith Wallerstein and Sandra Blakeslee's book
The Good Marriage: How and Why Love Lasts, the
authors explain that women often look for men who have
the qualities that they lack. When I read that, it rang a
bell. In my case, I believe that I was looking for a responsible grown-up. And there he was. My future fiancé strode
into our offices with his three-piece suit, sparkling Rolex,

and Hartman briefcase. He was the white-collar business executive personified. He pulled out his Montblanc pen and talked numbers so efficiently and effectively that my head was spinning. (Writers are bad at math.) He had a good job and was responsible.

Perfect. I could marry him. Never mind that his personality, worldview, and understanding of marriage were completely different from mine. And that's where my problems began.

It's Your Turn

Now comes the hard part. Ask yourself a series of questions that will help you understand why you are racing to the altar. Then decide what external pressures may be influencing you to get engaged to the wrong guy.

Why Do You Want to Get Engaged?

Have you carefully considered the following?

- Are you racing to the altar? Why do you want to get married?
- Will you want to marry this man six months from now?
- Do you think that everything will be "perfect" once you are actually married?
- Do you believe that your life will be instantly and magically happier once you utter your vows?

• Do you think marriage is a way out of your current loneliness, dead-end job, or personal doldrums?

• Are you getting married just because you think it is the next logical step in your courtship?

• If you are engaged, do you think you are getting married for the wrong reasons? Be honest.

• Do you and your boyfriend/fiancé share the same goals, beliefs, and ideals for your marriage?

• Have you even *talked* about any of this with him?

Are You Under Pressure?

Are you feeling pressured by any of the following?

• Do your parents think it's time for you to get married?

• Do your parents want you to marry your longtime boyfriend?

• Are your friends encouraging you to get married?

• Are your friends all getting married, so you want to get married, too?

• Has the age at which you always planned on getting married passed you by?

• Have you been dating the same person so long that you don't want to throw it all away, or feel like you have wasted that time?

• Is your biological clock ticking?

• Do you have it together in your work life but not in your personal life? Would marriage really solve this?

• Are you looking for financial security?

• Do you want to get out of your parents' house?

No one else knows the answers to these questions—
you. You must decide what you need for your life: Nam
discuss it, and do not give in to the external pressure to marry.
Pay attention to that little voice inside of you. Listen carefully to what it has to say. That is your "true self" talking, and
it has your best interests at heart.

✦　✦　✦　✦

How to Marry a Loving Man

- Date a man who treats you with respect.
- Choose a man who is a good friend to his friends and family.
- Fall in love with a man who respects all the women in his life.
- Seek a man who doesn't just talk the talk but walks the walk.

That way, when someone asks you what you love about him, you'll say:

My husband is honest, genuine, considerate, selfless, humble, and a great partner. These qualities benefit our marriage tremendously. In creating a good nurturing relationship, these qualities are essential. I value the person he is, and I try to be the best I can be in return.

✦

4

Needing More Than a
Pair of Warm Socks

Jitters and Cold Feet
During Engagement

*Love and doubt have never been on speaking
terms.*

—Kahlil Gibran

What's the Verdict: Cold Feet or Jitters?

Whenever we talk about a woman having doubts about her
pending marriage, people immediately start throwing around
the terms "jitters" or "cold feet." They use the terms inter-
changeably. "Everyone has jitters," they say. Or, "All brides
and grooms have cold feet before their weddings." We beg to
differ. While everyone might feel nervous about their wedding days, not all brides and grooms are concerned that they
may be making a mistake. We decided to look at the official
definitions of these terms for ourselves and settle the debate
once and for all.

According to *The American Heritage Dictionary:* "Jitters"
are defined as *nervousness; a feeling of fright or uneasiness.*

"Cold feet" is a slang term that means *fearfulness or timidity preventing the completion of a course of action.*

By definition, "cold feet" is more specific, as it relates to taking (or not taking) an action. Having the jitters means an overall sense of nervousness.

So how do you know if what you have are just normal prewedding jitters or if that frozen feeling in your feet is really trying to get you to run in the other direction?

- If you are feeling nervous or scared because you have temporary concerns about the event (the ceremony, reception, bridesmaids, family issues, etc.) you have the jitters.

- If you are feeling nervous or scared because you have questions about *the relationship itself,* then you have cold feet.

Jitters

Most brides will tell you that they experienced a bit of nervousness leading up to their wedding days:

- Will the florist show up on time?
- Will I stumble over my vows and embarrass myself?
- Will I cry?
- Will I faint at the altar?
- Will my little brother/aunt/uncle/cousin embarrass me at the wedding?
- Will the best man bring his new stripper girlfriend to the reception?
- And so on . . .

All are common concerns about the wedding and reception. These are planning issues, temporary concerns that revolve around the actual event itself, not the relationship.

Change can be a source of jitters.

Jitters also can stem from the tremendous change that is about to occur in your life. Going from single to married is a significant life change that should be met with some trepidation or fear. Just like the old quote says, "Living alone is like magic; all of your bad habits disappear." It's hard to give up your own space. As a single woman, you have the luxury of leaving your dirty clothes on the floor without being scolded. You have to worry about feeding only yourself. You can do whatever you want, whenever you want. You can hang a picture without having a two-hour discussion about where to put it! One way to better understand jitters is to look at other jitter-inducing events outside the context of marriage, such as

- A new job
- A completely different haircut
- College graduation
- A party where you don't know anyone
- A new puppy
- A start-up business

Just thinking about some of these things might make you nervous or fearful, but typically we face the fear and make a decision about whether we want to proceed. Without the issues of romance clouding our judgment, it's easier to make a decision—and sometimes that decision is a simple *no*.

Cold Feet

Having cold feet means that you have doubts about a pending action or transaction. Brides aren't the only ones who experience cold feet. Investors get cold feet. Home and car buyers get them, too. Cold feet before the wedding means that you are having reservations about getting married. Unfortunately, it's a lot easier to be cool and analytical about buying a house or car. When love and loneliness get thrown into the mix, that's where the trouble begins. When your feet feel cold—no matter what the circumstances—you need to pay attention. Any of the following thoughts about your pending marriage should be cause for concern:

- I feel like I am settling for him.
- I don't like how he treats me.
- I hope our relationship will improve after the wedding.
- I don't think he is going to be a good husband.
- I have to go through with this because we have been dating for so long.
- If I don't marry him, I will never find anyone else.

These thoughts revolve around the *relationship*, not the wedding ceremony or reception. These are not temporary issues, and they should not be ignored.

How Can I Tell the Difference?

Who better to offer insight on cold feet versus jitters than women who found the courage to call off their weddings? Here is how our brave panel diagnosed their cold feet:

I knew it wasn't prewedding jitters when everything in my mind, heart, and soul screamed that I was doing the wrong thing. In my previous relationship, my son's father and I talked about getting married (before the pregnancy occurred). I was on cloud nine. On my end, everything felt right with him. Unfortunately, he ended up feeling differently, so we never married. This time around, I was the one with the reservations. I think you just know *when it is right and when it is wrong. You have to listen to your gut.*

I recently married the right man, and I can tell you that this time I had no jitters on my wedding day. It was the happiest day of my life. When you are in a relationship with someone you are not truly happy with, it shows in every aspect of your life. When I called off my first wedding, I knew that I could not go through with something that I was not positive about. I could not lie to myself anymore and make it seem like I was happy in a relationship where I was really miserable.

I guess I knew it was cold feet when I kept thinking about calling off the wedding. Deep down I was concerned because I couldn't articulate what I really loved about him. It just became more and more clear that I was marrying him because of issues with myself and not because of our relationship.

I knew it was cold feet because I kept thinking, "How had I let it get this far—to the point of being married?" Why had I stayed in this relationship when I should have just gone out with him a few times and been done with it?

No jitters. Just deep down in my core miserable *when I was with him. It was pretty clear I had cold feet.*

By the time I called it off, I wasn't even thinking in terms of jitters or cold feet. When I confided in people, they tried to use these terms with me, to make me feel better. I knew it was more than jitters, and it was something I could not brush off as "normal" or "typical." I knew the relationship was wrong and that our marriage would not work. It was hard to face that.

Luckily we had not made any arrangements yet (because he was always too stressed out to talk about it), so there were no typical "prewedding jitters." However, I knew it was more than cold feet because after we decided to end our relationship, the first emotion I felt was relief. Of course I was sad, but more than anything I felt as if a weight had been lifted off my shoulders.

It was definitely not prewedding jitters. All of my reasons, and that feeling in my gut, were way bigger than nerves. This was the rest of my life we were talking about. I knew I didn't have commitment issues, just a hard time hurting someone who I purported to love so much. I really was more concerned with his feelings than with my own. I later learned that what I thought was love was really fear—fear of hurting him, fear of being alone, fear of what the future would hold for me without him.

❖   ❖   ❖   ❖

How to Marry an Angry Man

- Ignore his persistent sarcasm.
- Pay no attention to his job conflicts.
- Make excuses for why he doesn't work and play well with others.

That way, you will guarantee your family a life filled with conflict.

*I was so tired of his sarcastic humor with me and our sons. It was
mean-spirited. He was obsessed with keeping up with the Joneses.
He always had conflicts with neighbors, so we kept moving. He
never wanted to go out and do things. He had difficulty with all of
his jobs and was always blaming other people. He was sort of stuck
in his career. He was never going to follow a managerial track—
there was just too much conflict.*

✦

Conflicting Advice: Playing Alone in a Bad Neighborhood

In the course of researching this book, we went to several online wedding forums and message boards tagged with topics
such as "cold feet," "jitters," or "second thoughts." Two
things quickly became clear: First, there are a lot of people
trying to figure out the difference between jitters and cold
feet. They are desperate to figure out whether or not they
should call off their weddings. Second, there is a lot of conflicting (and sometimes scary) advice out there.

While online forums can be helpful, they also can be
akin to "playing alone in a bad neighborhood." The good
news is that you are reaching out for help. You're taking the
first step to address your concerns. But who are these people
offering advice on whether or not your concerns are normal?
What are their qualifications? The value of personal advice
from complete strangers can be questionable.

Another source of conflicting advice is the wealth of online articles available at the click of a mouse. If you do a quick Internet search on jitters or cold feet, you will find hundreds of articles. While some of the advice is right on target, other suggestions will leave a conflicted bride feeling even more confused. Written by well-meaning experts, the advice is often vague, with a one-size-fits-all approach. "Prewedding jitters are normal," they assure you. "Every bride or groom feels cold feet at some point." This may be true. Marriage is a huge transition. Change can be difficult. But there is a big difference between feeling nervous about the transition from single to married and having serious doubts about the relationship itself. And we believe that every woman knows deep down what she is feeling. Unfortunately, our overall impression is that most women are tempted to take this online advice, chalk up their feelings to jitters, and push aside their doubts. And as we have learned, when women ignore their intuition, they always regret it.

✦   ✦   ✦   ✦

Anne's Story: My Feet Were Ice Cold and Purple— and I Still Ignored Them

I was all alone in Chicago with my fiancé. I didn't have any friends, and I didn't have a job yet. I was in a state of limbo, and I was ignoring the warning bells ringing in my head. The only one who really acknowledged the tension was my cat, Ethel. She started spraying the walls around his dining room. She had never done this before. Disgusting, I know, but since she couldn't talk, she was trying to say, "Get out! What are you thinking? This is crazy!" My cat knew I was making a mistake and was telling me in her unique kitty way. I have no doubt that Ethel was responding to all of the stress and tension in the house. She knew I was unhappy.

As the days passed, it seemed like every time I turned around, I was smacked in the face with the mess I had gotten myself into. But for whatever reason I kept moving forward like some sort of passive robot. I was beyond questioning my cold feet or jitters. I knew we were completely incompatible. Our ideas about what marriage meant were so different. It was worse than that; neither of us had really formulated our own vision for what we believed marriage to be. I think we both thought that this was just the next step in our relationship. But I felt stuck. I was just trapped there, and I had no one to talk to about what I was feeling.

I went to look at wedding gowns one day and tried one on. I was depressed, sad, and sick to my stomach. It was zero fun—a chore. I can still see my reflection in the mirror. I felt like I was dressed up in a Halloween costume. I was all alone. There were several other groups of people at the bridal shop who were looking at dresses. They were having a grand old time—laughing, crying, and sharing a special moment. There were giddy bridesmaids, crying mothers, and joyful brides searching for that perfect dress.

And there I stood, all alone, thinking, "Damn, not only do I not want to marry him; I don't even think I *like* him."

✦

You Are Brave Enough to Face This!

When faced with a difficult decision, it's human nature to want to take the easy way out. If we are seeking advice on a problem, and we read several articles that assure us we are normal, we feel like we have permission to drop our concerns about the issue. That's why it's important to listen carefully to the one person who always knows what's right for you— and that's *you*. But how do you tackle such a difficult decision? Where do you begin?

Your Inner Voice Will Tell You Whether You Have Jitters or Cold Feet

Back to those gut feelings again! When grappling with jitters or cold feet, its best to turn to your inner voice. We all have conversations with ourselves.

"Those shoes are fabulous!"

"But you can't afford them right now."

"I know, but I should be getting that raise soon."

"You really need to save your money."

The part that wants you to have those shoes is probably the same part that is critical about how you dress, how you look and feel about yourself, how much more successful you would look if you just had those shoes. Your true self, that little voice in your head, knows that money is tight and you already have two maxed-out credit cards. Which voice do you listen to?

The same kind of dialogue goes on within us when we are in a relationship.

"He's really attractive."

"But he's not very respectful to other people."

"He's just really confident."

"No, he's arrogant."

"Well, he has a really stressful job and does not always have time to be nice to people."

"He's not very respectful to you."

"But he says he loves me and maybe he will change."

When we don't listen to our inner voices, we almost always get into trouble. By the time most of us heed the warning, we feel stuck, and we feel like it is too late to turn back. It is never too late!

You have a choice. What is your inner voice trying to warn you about? That voice inside of you—the core of who you are—is likely trying to warn you about your engagement or pending marriage. It's telling you that it's not just jitters. If anything in this book has made you sit up and say, "That's exactly how I feel!" then there's your answer. The answers you seek can be found in someone else's mistake. The people we interviewed spoke very candidly about the intimate details of their relationships. They have the benefit of hindsight and were willing to take a closer look. They can tell you what they did wrong—it's their gift to you. They knew they should have ended the relationship or called off the wedding, but something stopped them. What's stopping you?

✦   ✦   ✦   ✦

Jitters and Cold Feet: Not Just for Brides and Grooms!

Keep in mind that the concept of jitters and cold feet can be relevant even *before* you are engaged. It's helpful to apply these concepts to a boyfriend! If you find yourself feeling nervous or uncomfortable about your relationship, it's time to think about the red flag–gut feeling connection. For example, you and your boyfriend have planned a weekend getaway to the beach. You start to bicker over the arrangements, packing, departure times, and so on. You are upset because he is not returning your text messages and he becomes snippy when you finally get him on the phone. Do you think you two are bickering because you both have so many loose ends to tie up before you leave? Is it just temporary? Or deep down do you believe he is being rude and cranky because he is . . . well . . . rude and cranky? It's up to you to decide whether his moodiness is a temporary problem (jitters) related to your trip *or* whether your concerns are about his constant moodiness (cold feet).

✦

How Can I Be Sure?

So let's get back to the question we asked at the beginning of this chapter: Is it cold feet or jitters?

Take this quick multiple choice test and find out.

Q. You are feeling nervous about your wedding. Which of the following best describes the source of your concerns?

a. Planning the wedding and reception
b. Giving up my life as a single woman
c. Giving up my life as a single woman *and* the stress of planning the wedding and reception
d. My relationship with my fiancé

Your answer:___.

If you answered a, b, or c—it's probably just jitters. If you answered d, you most likely have cold feet. Now consider the following:

• What red flags are you seeing as the engagement and wedding plans progress? How are you feeling? What are your concerns? Are they related to the wedding planning or to the relationship?

• Imagine your life with him five years from now. How do you *really* see yourself? Will you be living an authentic life or will you just be pretending?

• Is he the wrong guy for you? Why or why not?

After working through these questions, how do you feel? Do you and your fiancé have permanent or temporary issues that are troubling you? Are you simply nervous, or do you have reservations that are preventing you from taking the next step . . . down the aisle? If you are still not sure, consider this: **If you could walk away right now and cancel the**

wedding, free of fear, free of guilt, free from embarrassment, and financially free, would you do it?

Be honest. If you would, then this is not "normal
prewedding jitters." You've got cold feet.

✦ ✦ ✦ ✦

How to Marry a Man Who Wants Only to Check You Off His To-Do List

- Ignore that voice that whispers, "He is marrying you to produce an heir."
- Dismiss his attraction to your Midwestern work ethic—and little else.
- Don't pay attention when deep down you don't feel loved and cherished.

That way, you'll be better able to accept your role as wife-for-hire.

It felt like I was another item to be checked off his "Life To-Do List" instead of someone he loved. He was at the point where it was time for him to say he had a wife, and he had to have a son. I was in my twenties so it was assumed I would be able to produce an heir— turns out that was not the case. He had gone to college in the Midwest and knew that he wanted a Midwestern wife because she would work hard and not demand too much from him.

✦

✦

PART 3

How
Not to Marry
the Wrong Guy

♦ 5 ♦

Sleepwalking into Marriage
Why Women Say "Yes" When the Wrong Guys Pop the Question

Marriage is miserable unless you find the right person that is your soul mate, and that takes a lot of looking.

—Marvin Gaye

Sleepwalking into Marriage

Hopefully our warnings about dating the wrong guy are starting to sink in. If you settle into a relationship with the wrong guy, you might find yourself—like so many other women we talked to—"passively pulled along" toward marriage. Others describe it as if they were "sleepwalking" or in a "surreal" state of being. One day they were stuck in a rut with the wrong guy, and the next thing they knew they were planning a wedding. At this point, the whole situation starts spinning out of control, and they are still "asleep"!

Charlotte Mayerson, the author of *Goin' to the Chapel: Dreams of Love, Realities of Marriage,* uses the term "sleepwalking" to describe how many women walk into a marriage without considering what kind of husband they need in order to have the kind of marriage they want. She interviewed women from across the United States, of all ages and walks of life, about how they viewed their married lives. Based on her extensive conversations, she identified two distinctly different attitudes that impacted the success and happiness of a marriage. She labeled these women as either "dreamers" or "calculators." According to Mayerson, the dreamers had not consciously outlined the characteristics that were important to them. She says these women usually had some vision for their married lives, but they did not quantify the type of men they needed to fulfill this vision.

For example, a young woman with a strong religious faith dreams of raising a large family in the suburbs. She pictures a life filled with church suppers, school activities, and plenty of family time. Her current boyfriend is an avowed agnostic who doesn't think he wants children. He loves his career as a stock trader and expects his wife to have a high-powered career, too. Do you think her dreams will be realized with this man? What about the woman who loves her fast-paced lifestyle? She pictures herself in a high-rise condominium in downtown Chicago. She can see her husband by her side as they explore everything the city has to offer— theaters, museums, and great restaurants. Don't you think she better think twice before marrying her current fiancé, a self-described homebody whose favorite pastime is hunting and fishing? These men are not going to change; neither are the women. Why should they? In the short term, these marriages might work; but in the long run, the odds are stacked against them.

The man you want to spend *your* life with is the man who shares a similar vision for the future. Waiting to pay attention to what you want out of your life together *after* you get married leads to . . . umm, well . . . *divorce.* Listen to these words of wisdom from a sixty-six-year-old self-described "dreamer" who was a part of Mayerson's study:

When it was time to get married, along came this guy who was handsome and a great athlete—just like my dopey dreams. So I married him. I never thought about it in terms of what life was all about. I didn't say, "Is he going to make a good husband? Are we going to have a good life together? Do we have the same ideals? Will he be able to earn a living? Be proud of himself?" None of that. Absolutely none.*

After so many tales of divorce from the dreamers, Mayerson's undeniable conclusion is that the majority of women who failed to consider the qualities they desired in a husband had unhappy first marriages. On the flip side, the women who *did* qualify what they wanted in a husband—the calculators—were much more likely to have a happy marriage.

Being described as a "calculating woman" can be perceived as negative. But what it actually means is that you have practically and thoughtfully considered all of the important characteristics you desire in your future spouse or in

*Charlotte Mayerson, *Goin' to the Chapel: Dreams of Love, Realities of Marriage* (New York: BasicBooks, 1996), 32.

a long-term relationship. It also means that you have thought about your vision for your married life. If it takes being labeled a calculator to build a happy and satisfying marriage or relationship, wear that label with pride. It will lead you to take a long, hard look at whether your current boyfriend or fiancé meets those qualifications. It will also give you the facts you need in order to recognize whether a relationship will work (and the courage to end it if it won't).

✦   ✦   ✦   ✦

Anne's Story: How Diana, Princess of Wales, Helped Me Make Up My Mind and Cancel My Wedding

Legend has it that Princess Diana wanted to cancel her wedding to Prince Charles . . . but something stopped her. I thought about this as I pulled one thick and luxurious monogrammed towel after another out of a gift box. My heart sank when I took a second look at the monogrammed his-and-her Polo robes. Picked just for me at the Ralph Lauren store in Palm Beach, this gift was very generous—and nonreturnable.

I was unpacking wedding gifts at my fiancé's home. They were from an elaborate going-away party / wedding shower held in my honor a few weeks prior.

It was a catered affair with all of my favorite foods. I received dozens of wonderful gifts. But by the time these gifts arrived, I already knew I wanted to call off the wedding. As I unpacked each one, I felt progressively more nauseous. I thought of all the nice people who had carefully selected these presents just for me. I considered all the planning that went into the party and how much fun it was. I reflected on how happy everyone seemed to be for me. I can clearly remember thinking, "It's too late to call off the wedding because the towels have already been monogrammed."

That jolted another memory that really resonated. I remembered a quote that had been attributed to Princess Diana's sister. In the weeks leading up to the royal wedding, Great Britain was abuzz at the fairy tale in the making, and there were all manner of commemorative souvenirs for sale. When the former Diana Spencer told her sisters Sarah and Jane that she wanted to call off the wedding, one of them said, "Too late, Duch [the family name for Diana], your face is already on the tea towels." Just like my big box of mono-grammed towels. "*Too late,*" I thought. "*The towels are already monogrammed.*"

Somehow I came to my senses. I decided then and there that I wasn't going to let a gift of monogrammed towels get in the way of my happiness. Even though a part of me was afraid that this was my one and only chance to get married, I knew that I wasn't about to marry a prince. And he certainly didn't treat me like his future queen. I didn't want to end up like poor Princess Diana. Just like that, I made up my mind that I was going to call off my wedding. And I felt better immediately.

I did keep the monogrammed towels, though. In fact, I just threw the last one out about a year ago. They were fabulous. I used them every day. The only problem was I would occa-sionally have to explain to my guests why my towels had an unfamiliar monogram. I can't help it if I'm practical!

✦

Why Do They Feel Pressured to Say Yes?

A relationship does not have to include dishonesty, infidelity, or disrespect to be wrong. Two perfectly wonderful people can be in a relationship and simply be wrong *for each other.* We heard it again and again. "That little voice kept telling me this was all wrong, but I struggled with ending it because he was a good person." Or, "He had so many good qualities, but I just didn't feel that spark." This seems to be a major source of confusion and anxiety. Women talk themselves out of what they know is right. They are conflicted about breaking up with nice boyfriends, even though the electricity or chemistry is missing. They tell themselves that they should stay because their partners are not cheaters or liars. There's no drama (which is a good thing), but deep down they know that the relationship is not all that it should be.

I think I knew from the moment he proposed that it was wrong. I couldn't say no because he had proposed in such a public way that I didn't have the heart to humiliate him, so I said yes. Then once the "yes" was out of my mouth, I felt like there was no turning back. He was so happy, and I, on the other hand, didn't even want to call my parents! The deeper I got into the planning, the harder it was; the deposits were made, and the dress was purchased. I felt like I would be a fool if I called it off, but still, it just didn't feel right. I felt sick to my stomach more often than not. I battled with myself: Which scenario was worse, going through with it or calling it off?

It defies logic to get engaged when deep down you really don't want to marry him. So why say yes when he pops the question? It's almost always one of the following three reasons:

1. They don't want to let everyone down or hurt their fiancés' feelings.

2. They fear this will be their one and only chance to get married.

3. They have invested too much time in the relationship.

1. They don't want to let everyone down or hurt their fiancés' feelings.

Starting at a very young age, we are taught to be kind to others and to consider their feelings. It's true that the golden rule is important. However, when you put everyone else's feelings ahead of your own, it becomes a problem—especially when it comes to canceling your wedding.

I felt so guilty—I did not want to let everyone down. What is interesting is that I know that my parents would have totally supported me. All of my energy was directed at finishing school at that point, so I just went ahead with it because I couldn't deal with that particular problem at the time.

People who really love you will not be angry when you tell them that your relationship and wedding are over. They may express concern or dismay, but they want you to be happy and will support you. You must remind yourself that you and you alone are the only person who will be married to your future spouse. So you need to decide whether he is right for you. His family may be upset and disappointed. They may be angry. Remember—it is *your* life, and you must take charge of it. If the relationship does not feel right or your fiancé does not cherish or respect you, call it off. In this case you must put *your* feelings ahead of everyone else's.

I loved his whole family. So did my parents. We all got along so well. It was like breaking up with his mom and dad and three sisters, too. But deep down, I knew the right thing for me was to call it off. I knew our marriage wouldn't work in the long run.

Another woman who *wished* she had canceled said:

The ironic part is that my mom would have completely supported me if I had. In fact, she gave me ample opportunity to cancel the wedding. She carefully broached the subject with me in a nonthreatening manner. But for some reason, I didn't listen.

One woman who did gather up the courage to call off her wedding described the day she told her fiancé it was over:

When I tried to talk to my fiancé about the problems I was having with the relationship, he was so disconnected. We didn't see eye to eye. In his mind, there were no problems. And that was the problem. His idea of what a good relationship looked like was so completely different from mine. The day I told him I was leaving he went out and cut the grass. Then he came back in and yelled at me a little bit. Then he went out and washed my car and then came back and yelled a little bit more. He told me I was ungrateful and that I had unrealistic expectations. I remember thinking, "No, it's just that I had better marital role models in my parents. You don't see how poorly your dad treats your mother."

I left and spent the night at a hotel with my parents, who had driven in from out of town to help me gather my things. I went back to his house after he had gone to work the next morning and got the rest of my stuff. I got in my car and headed for my hometown nine hours away.

I didn't hear from him for two weeks. My dad expressed dismay that he didn't even try to "woo me back." I was full blast into my new life. I got a new job within days, I leased an apartment, and I was really happy. I was so relieved—I felt like the weight of the world was off my shoulders. When he finally called me he said, "Hi, honey. Are you ready to come back?" He was clueless—he still didn't understand that it was over. I told him, "I really meant this—we are through. I have a new job and a yearlong lease. Pack up any odds and ends you find of mine around the house and send them back to me." That was that.

That was sixteen years ago, and I still get a warm and fuzzy feeling thinking about leaving him. It brings a smile to my face when I talk about it. I was so glad I had the courage to call it off . . . to recognize what a huge mistake it was. Yes, it was embarrassing, but the freedom and relief far outweighed any embarrassment.

I am so glad I listened to that little voice in my head that was screaming at me to call it off. I put my feelings first, and it ended up being one of the smartest, bravest things I have ever done.

2. They fear that this will be their one and only chance to get married.

Many women were afraid to call off their weddings because they thought it was their only chance to marry. For whatever reason: They were getting older, they couldn't picture anyone else, or they were in a rut. They thought that they *had* to go through with the marriage, or they would end up alone.

I wondered if anyone else would want to marry me . . . if there would ever be another person that I would want to marry.

I believed that he was the best I could get.

I thought he was so good-looking. I never thought that I would get the chance to marry someone like him.

What is ironic is that everyone we interviewed has gone on to a much happier life. Even more telling is that most of their lives have taken wonderful twists and turns beyond their imagining.

I remember sitting all alone on the couch in his house wondering what I should do. I knew I had to call it off, but I was scared. I was twenty-nine years old and couldn't imagine meeting another man. It's sad, but I didn't want to be alone. All of my friends were married. However, I was smart enough to know that I was better off alone than in an unhappy relationship. I didn't like my options—but I called it off. I am so glad I did!

One thing I always tell people who are in a rut, or depressed about their current life situation, is that you never know where your life is headed next. I couldn't have dreamed up what happened to me in the years after I called off my wedding. I got a great job, found a great guy (I wasn't looking), and ended up getting married. We have three wonderful kids, and I never looked back. I could barely see out of the hole I was in at the time—but I had enough faith in myself to call it off.

Too many people get married because they have put blinders on—they see only what is right in front of them. They have limited their possibilities. Like the woman whose story we've just seen, you must have faith in yourself! There is something better out there for you and it may or may not include getting married.

3. They have invested too much time in the relationship.

It was amazing to see how many women fell into the "wasted time" trap. Saying you'll marry the wrong guy because you don't want to waste the time you have invested in the relationship doesn't make sense. It's like throwing good money after bad. We were shocked to hear this repeated by so many women:

We had dated for several years. I didn't want to waste that. It was like it was too late to turn back the clock.

I was young, I wanted the dream wedding, and we had invested what I believed at the time to be sooooo many years into the relationship.

We had been together for so long. I didn't want to throw all those years of my life away.

I felt I owed him—we had been together for several years, and he had stayed with me during my cancer treatments.

A few years wasted in a bad relationship won't seem so long in the big picture of your life. What about the time wasted in a bad marriage? Stop the clock and say no.

Did You Say, "Yes, I'll Marry You" for Any of the Following Reasons?

- You don't want to let everyone down or hurt your fiancé's feelings.
- You are afraid that this will be your one and only chance to get married.
- You believe that you have invested too much time in the relationship, and you don't want to waste all that time spent together.

If you agreed to get married for *any* of these reasons, it's time to rethink your engagement. The good news is that it's not too late to call it off!

With This Ring, I Thee Dread
Why Women Say "I Do" When They're Thinking "I Don't!"

If you marry the wrong person for the wrong reasons, then no matter how hard you work, it's never going to work, because then you have to completely change yourself, completely change them, completely—by that time, you're both dead.

—Anne Bancroft

Blinded by the White Dress

Once a woman gets engaged, she is on a fast track down the aisle. The focus shifts from the ring to the party. It's all about the dress, the flowers, the food, and the festivities. The pressure multiplies. Unfortunately, all of that pressure can force a woman to say "I do" when she wants to say "I don't!" One woman we talked to summed it up this way:

I was so blinded by my white dress, cake, invitations, limo, and plans for the ceremony that I couldn't think straight.

She's not alone! After talking to hundreds of women who wanted to say, "No, no, I really don't," we uncovered the three most common reasons that they walk down that aisle anyway.

1. They are caught up in the momentum of the wedding; it was too late to call it off.

2. They are afraid of publicly admitting a mistake; they feel shame and embarrassment.

3. They feel like it is too expensive to cancel the wedding.

1. They are caught up in the momentum of the wedding; it was too late to call it off.

Many women said that they were so caught up in the momentum of the wedding plans that it was too late to call it off. This is simply not true. It is never too late.

My whole life revolved around our wedding plans. That's all everyone talked to me about. I felt like there was no turning back.

Everything was organized, the party was planned, and everyone was looking forward to the wedding. (Everyone but me, that is.)

I did want to call off the wedding, but I just felt swept along. I wanted to keep everyone happy.

Several women said they felt they had passed the point of no return once they received that first wedding gift or attended their first shower. Wrong! Don't let your wedding gifts paralyze you. A pile of beautifully wrapped gifts does not have the power to keep you from canceling your wedding. You don't want a set of wineglasses or a wok to dictate your future.

The organist can have her fingers poised over the keyboard, and you can still pull the plug. One woman called her wedding off in the wee hours of the morning after the rehearsal dinner:

So, I hung up the phone and drove to the spa to meet my bridesmaids; some were already getting their nails done. One stopped at my car and asked if I was coming in. . . . I burst into tears and had to explain it was being postponed or called off. It was quite a sight when four girls ran out the door with their shoes off and toes partially painted.

It wasn't easy, but she didn't regret it. It was the right thing to do. Six months, six weeks, six days, six hours, six minutes beforehand . . . if it is not right now it won't work in the long run. It's never too late to call it off.

2. They are afraid of publicly admitting a mistake; they feel shame and embarrassment.

It's never pleasant to make a mistake—particularly a very public one. Countless women told us that embarrassment kept them from calling off their weddings:

I did not want to admit I had made a huge mistake, and I kept thinking I could make things work.

I did not want the embarrassment of calling off a planned wedding.

Two things stopped me from calling it off. The first was pride—I did not want to admit that my parents were right (they had never liked my fiancé), and I did not want to admit I had made a mistake.

There is no getting around the fact that if you call off your wedding, you will have to admit to everyone in your life you made a mistake. You'll have to tell your friends, neighbors, coworkers, and hairdresser (the list goes on). But think about this: Once you admit this, it is over and done with. You admit you made a mistake, and that's that. It is out there in the open. Sure, a few people might snicker behind your back. But your real friends and loving family members will support you. They will be proud of you for having the courage to call it off.

I told a lot of family and friends. It was the most embarrassing thing I ever had to do. I had already had a bridal shower with all of my mom's friends. I already had my dress. The thing that was a relief was that no one gave me any trouble about calling it off. Later, I became a little angry at family and friends for not saying something to me sooner!

Don't forget: If you get a divorce, you'll still have to do the *exact same thing*. You'll still have to admit you made a mistake. Save yourself the trouble. How's this for embarrassing?

He didn't show up at court for our divorce. His mother was a legal secretary, so she replaced him. I had to tell the court (in front of the entire courtroom) that because he had been unfaithful to me, I had been given a venereal infection. I was very embarrassed, but my wonderful sister-in-law (my brother's wife) gave me support at court.

Sure, there may be a few folks who tell you that canceling your wedding is a big mistake. They may even try to talk you out of it. But what do they know? The gut feelings belong to you—no one else.

On the whole, you will be surprised how supportive most people will be. Everyone we interviewed who had called off a wedding received tremendous support.

My parents told me they supported me 100 percent—and so did the rest of my family. Evidently, all my siblings and even my aunts, uncles, and cousins who had met him had had major concerns.

✦   ✦   ✦   ✦

People Who "Always" Make Mistakes and People Who "Never" Make Mistakes

There are some women who try to never make mistakes, and other women who feel they always make mistakes. They both gave the same reason for going ahead with their weddings: *They didn't want to make a mistake.* We had a big lightbulb moment when we repeatedly heard statements like this:

I had observed my sister making many mistakes and getting in a lot of trouble. I didn't want to do anything wrong. I never did anything wrong. I felt I couldn't call it off—that would be the "wrong" thing to do.

I had made a whole series of public and painful mistakes in my early twenties, one of which was running away to the country, getting pregnant, and marrying a good-for-nothing guy. I had three kids with him and spent years getting my life on track. I was preparing to finally remarry—a really nice guy, but a guy I knew was wrong for me. As the day was getting closer, I wanted to cancel. But I just couldn't. I felt like I had made so many mistakes in the past—I didn't want to raise that whole issue again. I didn't want to risk making another public mistake. So I went through with it.

Everyone makes mistakes. It's okay to admit when you are wrong. Nobody's perfect—perfect people do not exist on this earth. There are only people who *think* they are perfect, and they are incredibly annoying. So admit your mistake. It's better to face up to a mistake beforehand instead of going through with one to save face.

◆

3. They feel it is too expensive to cancel the wedding.
There's no question that there are short-term costs associated with canceling your wedding. But remember, there are many more nasty, unpleasant, and complicated long-term costs associated with *not* canceling your wedding. The fact is, if you cancel your wedding, you are going to lose some money. Deposits on everything from the reception location, the band,

the caterer, the flowers, the cake, and so forth, may be gone forever. Take the time to add it all up and see what it will really cost you so you will never second-guess yourself. Determine what the exact number will be. Let's look at a hypothetical wedding:

$1,500	deposit on reception location
$500	deposit for florist
$3,500	nonreturnable wedding gown
$500	deposit to hold the date for the band
$1,250	plane tickets for honeymoon
$7,250	

So the bad news is that this bride knows she will lose $7,250 by canceling the wedding. That is the bottom-line number. Yikes, that sure seems like a lot of money, but think about the costs of splitting your assets in half, hiring a $250-an-hour divorce attorney, and being responsible for half of your ex-spouse's debts.

I canceled my wedding six months to the day beforehand. I had not purchased my wedding dress yet, or thought out a lot of the details. In fact, that was one of my red flags: I kept putting off the wedding planning because I knew that I didn't want to go through with it. Fortunately, the only money I lost was the $1,500 deposit on the reception location. I consider it $1,500 well spent!

The good news is that if you get on the phone immediately and clearly and rationally explain the situation to your wedding vendors, there is a chance that you can get some of your money back. If the reception site gets booked after you cancel, they may even consider refunding all of your money.

Another woman spent years paying off debt from her canceled wedding:

My parents told me they would help me with whatever financial implications there were [for calling it off]. It cost approximately $40,000 to break off the engagement. I felt strongly that since it was my choice and not my fiancé's to break the engagement, I needed to pay for these expenses. I was working at a nonprofit at the time and not making much money, so this was a huge step for me. It made me realize I really wanted to do this. It took me five years to reimburse my parents.

Even after all that, she was *still* glad she called it off.

✦   ✦   ✦   ✦

How to Marry a Head Case

- Ignore his checkered job history.
- Make excuses for why he drinks too much.
- Allow yourself to be easily manipulated.

That way, you won't be surprised when he cheats on you.

He had a very public affair. Everyone was aware of it and talked about it. I could no longer pretend. There was so much else going on, though. He was drinking too much, and he had had nine jobs in the twelve years we had been married. He had also been unemployed several times. Life was tough even before I knew about the affair. I filed for divorce once, and he came back very hard core again. He said to me, "How can you do this to our children and not give it one more try?" He always knew what to say to get me to cave. He then proceeded to have another affair with a girl who was twenty years younger. Then I was ready. It was a big paradigm shift for me. I truly believed I would never be divorced—that I would never do that to my children.

✦

You Never Know How It Will Turn Out

This brave woman canceled her wedding when she realized her fiancé was having doubts about their pending marriage:

After about three years of dating, I realized that he really just couldn't commit, so I broke up with him. We went our separate ways for several months and then he wanted to get back together. He said he loved me and missed me and wanted to get married. He promised me he was 100 percent ready. I loved him and trusted him, but even as I accepted his proposal, somewhere deep down inside I had doubts. We planned a wedding for six months later. About two months before the wedding, I quit my job and moved across the country to be with him. I sold my furniture at a garage sale and basically got rid of everything I owned in preparation for our life together.

Soon after moving, she realized that he was once again having doubts. (We will hear more from this wise almost-bride in chapter 8.) She ultimately called off her wedding just two weeks before the big day.

The wedding was planned for only about 120 guests—not huge. After he called my family and my bridesmaids, my friends and family did a phone chain for my guests, and my ex-fiancé took care of calling all of his guests. He returned the gifts that had been sent to us with notes of apology. I was paralyzed, pretty much in la-la land. Thankfully, my family took over.

My mom called all the venues to cancel and tried her best to negotiate the band, florist, and photographer out of their cancellation fees. We did lose all of the deposits. My fiancé later reimbursed my parents for these expenses. My dad added up all the expenses that people were out, including the deposits my parents had lost, bridesmaid dresses that had been purchased, my teacher's salary for six months, and the furniture that had been sold so cheaply at a garage sale. He prepared a letter requesting reimbursement [from my ex-fiancé]. I also kept the engagement ring (at my fiancé's suggestion) that was worth roughly $10,000. I later sold it and used the money as a down payment on my first house. I can't remember the total amount that he reimbursed, but I would guess that it was around $30,000.

At the time, some people remarked that it was incredible that he did all of that, because he didn't have to. But it was what he had *to do to clean up his mess. I believe it was absolutely fair and the right thing to do. The fact that my sister was involved in a serious relationship with his brother—and he didn't want to cause strife there—undoubtedly helped me garner that financial support from him. I don't know if he would have done what was fair and right if that had not been the case.*

Fortunately, her fiancé took full financial responsibility for the cancellation of their wedding. What if she had let these financial issues keep her from doing what was right for her? She would have missed out on the great guy she married several years after she called off this wedding—that's what! Her story proves that you *never* know what your future holds—and you won't find out if you let money keep you from calling it off.

Are you still not convinced to call it off? Then perhaps this woman's cautionary tale will sway you:

I Said "I Do" When I Should Have Said "I Don't": One Bride's Story of Her Courtship, Marriage, and Divorce

This bride was a smart, beautiful, and capable woman who had a successful and lucrative career. Here is what she told us about her relationship before the wedding:

He lived with his parents at the age of twenty-seven with no intention of moving out. His mother issues were a huge red flag. All of his friends kept asking me, "What does his mom think?" after we got engaged. I also heard from several of his friends that his mom never left his side. In college, she used to hang out in his dorm room when he wasn't even there.

His mother was crazy as a loon. This really came out when she drank. His family loved to party, and most every evening fell apart once the cocktails began to flow. But his mom had problems beyond the love of the drink. We played on a coed softball team, and he also played on the men's team. His parents showed up at almost every game with their cooler and lawn chairs. They would cheer from the sideline like he was still an eight-year-old Little Leaguer. At first, I thought it was nice that they joined us, but hanging out at our softball games turned into hanging out at a pub on Friday night, and going to the wineries on Sundays.

I was in my midtwenties; I wanted to pal around with friends our age. Going out every weekend with his parents got old quickly, especially when the drinking started and my soon-to-be mother-in-law's whole persona changed. Once she had a few drinks, she got this crazy look in her eye and began hurling all sorts of insulting comments that basically insinuated that nobody was good enough for her son! I was so tired of this behavior that I refused to drink anymore whenever we were around them. One evening at the regular Friday night pub outing, she leaned across the table and clearly stated, "It's been so long since I saw Mr. Pee Pee." Immediately, my fiancé leaned across the table, pointed his finger at her, and told her to shut up!

She wanted to call off her wedding, but she didn't. What stopped her?

I knew I had big problems, but I thought I could get past them. All of my friends were already married and I was determined to get married. . . . I was determined to make this work.

She was also concerned about her parents' money:

My parents were comfortable but not affluent. They worked really hard for their money. I knew they had already spent about $4,500 on the wedding, and I didn't have the heart to call it off and make them lose their money.

There were all sorts of red flags associated with the wedding festivities:

At our engagement party at my sister's house, his mom showed up with purple hair; she was already drunk. My sister had a beautiful house, and his mom rolled out of the car and said, "Who do these people think they are?" She was critical of the home, the affluence. My two aunts later told me that they had witnessed his mom stop my future husband at the bottom of the steps and give him a bizarre kiss, not a mother-son kiss. A kiss on the mouth! At another point during the night she laughed and red wine came out of her nose. At our rehearsal dinner she asked one of the groomsmen to talk my fiancé out of the wedding, saying it was the biggest mistake he would ever make. He said that it was not his place and immediately told my future husband and me. She was very close to his best man, and at the wedding someone overheard him actually call me a cunt!

She talked herself into thinking that things would get better after the marriage.

Even before the wedding I told myself I did not want to have children with him because I did not want to bring them up in that strange, alcoholic environment. For some reason I thought everything would change after we got married.

She didn't listen to that little voice that knew better, the one that wanted to call off the wedding. When did she realize the gravity of her mistake?

Two weeks after the wedding we went out to the wineries with some friends, and of course we ran into his parents. His mom was showing some pictures of the wedding to their friends, and I mentioned something about the best man calling me a nasty name at the wedding. His mom blew a gasket. She said to me, "You deserve it. You are a bitch." I turned on her and said, "You have no right to say that—just as you had no right to try to break up our wedding." I knew this wasn't going to be good, and I kept thinking I should flip on my video camera that was sitting next to me. I wish I would have because she twisted the entire story and stormed out, telling everyone I had called her a cunt! I was devastated. Two weeks into my marriage and she had turned their entire family against me.

My husband was miserable about the rift between his mother and me. I did attempt to have a normal marriage but he never wanted to have sex. I think it happened seven times in total during the eleven months we were married. That was fine with me, because there was no way I was going to get pregnant. I did not want to have kids with him. I went through the motions of throwing him a thirtieth birthday party. A group of my college friends pulled me aside and asked, "How long are you going to do this?" Eight months after our wedding, we were set to celebrate our first Christmas together. He went out to see his family (I was not welcome; in fact, I never spoke to them again after the winery incident), and he was supposed to meet me later that afternoon at my aunt's house. He never showed up. I was really embarrassed. My cousins were teasing me. They said, "Where's your husband?" It wasn't in a mean way, but they all knew that it was odd that he never came back from his mother's house. Eventually, I started having terrible headaches. I was convinced I had a brain tumor. I went and had an MRI. Nothing showed up. One day while driving home from a business trip, I glimpsed in the rearview mirror and saw my jaw clenched so tight; I had TMJ. I was a total stress case. I looked awful—just a monstrous physical mess. This marriage was taking a terrible physical toll on me.

Eleven months after the wedding, she wrote him a Dear John letter and ended the relationship.

He went straight home to mama. He started getting really nasty about all of the money. I knew he was being coached by his mother. We had to split up our assets, and I bought his share of the house. Instead of using the money as a down payment on another home, he moved back in with his parents and bought a sports car. He wanted to go back to school and wanted me to pay his tuition! I was furious. I threatened to raise the alcohol abuse issues in the family and his mother issues in divorce court. He walked away. I heard through the grapevine, many years later, that nothing has changed. It's not my problem anymore.

She endured emotional abuse from him and his family. She developed physical problems as a result of all the tension, and she narrowly missed giving him half of her hard-earned assets. It would have been a lot easier to cancel the wedding in the first place. Hindsight is 20/20. She shares this painful story with you so you don't make the same mistake. If you have serious reservations about your relationship, take a step back and carefully evaluate what is best for you. Don't be tricked by the issues of unplanning a party. Determine whether your gut is telling you to end your unstable relationship. Deal with those feelings first. After you acknowledge the need to end the relationship, you can deal with the ins and outs of canceling a party.

This bride later went on to marry a great guy. She had a small, beautiful wedding and has wonderful in-laws with whom she has a solid, loving relationship. They are happily married and have three lovely daughters. She and her husband share the same goals for their family life and enjoy spending time on sports, school activities, travel, and all the other fun that comes with being a family. She says she's learned a lot from her mistake and has made sure to apply those painful lessons to her second marriage.

✦   ✦   ✦   ✦

How to Marry an Emotionally Abusive Man

- Ignore his self-centered behavior.
- Don't pay attention to your friends when they warn you about his cheating ways.
- Deny the fact that he is emotionally abusive.
- Convince yourself that he will change after you are married.

That way, you won't be surprised when your married life turns out like this:

Throughout our marriage he was a real jerk. He was verbally and physically abusive. When we returned from our honeymoon, the honeymoon was really over. He would not help with any of the household chores, wouldn't even pick his plate up from the table. He would go out and party with his friends when he was supposed

to be home, or when he was supposed to meet up with me he
would be several hours late. He had three different affairs within
the ten years of our marriage and denied them all, even when
I had hard facts. He was a lazy, bald-headed, dishonest jerk who
I had wasted eighteen years of my life with. The final straw was
when I found out he had been sleeping with the seventeen-year-old
babysitter for two years. I asked him to give her up because we
had a two-year-old daughter. He said no.

◆

Are You Going to Say "I Do" for Any of the Following Reasons?

- You are too caught up in the momentum of the wedding and think it's too late to call it off.
- You are afraid of publicly admitting a mistake and want to avoid the shame and embarrassment of canceling your wedding.
- The potential financial losses of a canceling the wedding are preventing you from calling it off.

If you answered yes to even one of the above, you are headed down the aisle to disaster. The good news is that it's not too late to call it off!

- Write down the reasons you are forging ahead with your wedding plans.
- Are they similar to the reasons found in this chapter? Are they temporary reasons? Do they make sense?

This woman found the courage to call off her first wedding and shares why it was the best decision she ever made:

I had gone through every scenario in my head, and I realized that I could not go through with something that I was not 100 percent sure of. I did not want to put my family through the heartache of having a wedding and then it not working out. I knew when I did get married that I wanted it to be forever, and I just did not see forever with him. (By the way, I just got married on October 25, 2008. I married my best friend, and I couldn't be happier—I believe that everything happens for a reason.)

Need more convincing? The next chapter will show you why you are better off alone than married to the wrong guy.

✦

PART 4

How
to Break Up
with the Wrong Guy

✦ 7 ✦

I Don't Want to Be Alone
Are You Better Off with the Wrong Guy or
Are You Better Off Alone?

*You did the best that you knew how. Now that
you know better, you'll do better.*

—Maya Angelou

Why Do Smart Women Stay with the Wrong Guys?

The main reason women settle for dead-end relationships is that *they are afraid of being alone*. That fear drives them to ignore red flags and gut feelings about their relationships and avoid the daunting task of breaking up.

What would happen if you took the energy you are spending hanging on to the wrong guy and created an open space in your life to attract the right guy? Travel, try new things, explore new ways of doing things, and—through your experiences—you might meet the right guy. And if you don't, that's OK, too. You don't need to be in a relationship to be happy and fulfilled!

We have talked to hundreds of women from across the country who stayed with and eventually married men who were wrong for them. After they escaped their unhappy marriages, they found they were grateful to be alone. It is unfortunate that they had to suffer through miserable marriages and painful divorces to value being alone. Let's look at some of the objections that might keep you from ending a less-than-satisfying relationship:

- Age
- Hurt feelings
- Thinking he'll change
- Settling
- Divorce
- Financial fears

Age: "I wanted to have kids before the age of thirty. If I break up with him, I might not have a chance to have children because I will be too old."

We are not sure how the magic age of thirty became the deadline for getting married and having children, but we heard this one a lot. Wanting to have a baby is simply not a good reason to marry the wrong guy. Children are *never* the answer to your problems. If he is not a good boyfriend, then why would he make a good father? If you think life is complicated now, add a baby with colic and reflux, diminished sleep, and increased financial pressure to the equation. What kind of guy will he be then? If having a child is truly that important to you, wouldn't you want to wait to share the monumental task of raising a child with someone who will actually be able to step up to the plate? Don't get married just because your self-imposed biological clock is starting to tick a little louder. We met plenty of women who waited to have children with the right guy. Many of them were in their late thirties or even early forties, and their age did not affect the happy families they created. There are all sorts of ways to become a mother, and you don't have to marry the wrong guy to do it!

When I got married at the age of thirty-nine, I had no fears about being an "older" mom. I had faith that I would become a mother in one way or another. Now that I have my daughter, I feel more confident than many of the younger moms I see at the playground. I am also calmer! I think it's because I had the chance to grow up myself before I had kids.

✦   ✦   ✦   ✦

How to Marry a Manipulative Man

- Make excuses for why he "embellishes" his résumé.
- Ignore the fact that he arranged the theft of his own car.
- Don't pay attention to his nicotine-stained teeth and fingers.
- Look the other way whenever he breaks a promise.

That way, you won't be surprised when your life gets caught up in his web of deceit.

When we were dating, his car was stolen. He then told me he had arranged to have it stolen to collect the insurance money. He smoked and lied about it. He was manipulative and did not keep his promises. He also lied about graduating from college. He got a job

that did not require a diploma, or a transcript. He lied to his
employers. It was never-ending.

✦

Hurt feelings: "I don't want to hurt him. He needs me."
As women, our role in the world has always been to take care
of others. Breaking up with a man defies that role. In a sense,
we give up our wants and desires to maintain the status quo.
In the meantime, your boyfriend is sleeping with other
women, lying to you about sleeping with other women, and
making you feel bad about yourself because he is sleeping
with other women. Sure, he needs you: He needs you to be a
doormat! As Dr. Phil would say, "How is that working out
for you?" Here is a story from a woman we interviewed who
is *still* in a relationship with the wrong guy. She knows it's
wrong, yet she can't let go because she is more concerned
with what he needs than what she wants or needs for herself.

I am actually currently dating the wrong guy and have stayed
for a multitude of illogical reasons. When I first started dating
my boyfriend, I had "the feeling"—the one that everyone says,
"When you meet the right one, you'll just know." Well, every-
thing felt perfect, and I was sure we would make it. I'm usually
very logical in relationships, so this was unusual for me. He was
older, he was respected by everyone I knew, and he was just so in-
teresting. He had done a lot of international volunteer work
that I admired. However, as time wore on, I started noticing
things about him that were not at all compatible with me. He is
emotional and dependent. He is smart and adventurous, so he
sees the world as a sea of options and has a hard time deciding

what he wants to do. Then, when he decides, he has a hard time sticking with it. I come from a stable household, and I know I would have a hard time being patient and understanding with his life decisions. I question his ability to support me and any family we might have.

Also, he seems to care more about his adventures and his life than he does about mine. He always has noble, respectable excuses to miss these events in my life, but I can't help thinking that he's not going to be there for most of the big milestones in my life because he'll be too busy with his own adventures.

It's now been two and a half years since we originally started dating, and I'm still with him. I've known for sure that we aren't right for each other off and on throughout that time, and I'm sure right now that I need to end it for good. It's just hard, because I'm always thinking that it's not the right time or that he needs my support. He's struggling with trying to decide whether to volunteer for a yearlong deployment in Afghanistan, and he's leaning on me for support. I can't help but think that if he was really into me the way he should be, he wouldn't be volunteering to leave me again for a year and put our life on hold.

I think if I really felt for him like I needed to, I'd be fighting it more. He says he just wants to get one last adventure out of the way before he settles down, but I don't think that will be enough for him. We hardly ever talk about the future or getting married, which I think is rare for people who have been together for as long as we have. I really want someone who can't wait to marry me, and he isn't it. I think it's just hard to let go of those original feelings I had for him, and I keep hoping that they will come back someday.

As of publication of this book, she is still with this guy. We wish she weren't. She is hanging on to the hope that someday the old feelings she had for him will return. This is another common reason women stay in bad relationships.

Thinking he'll change: "He is going to change. He was so great when we started dating; I know that person is still inside of him."
But is that who he *really* is? We are typically on our best behavior when we first meet someone. If he acts one way at the beginning of your relationship but you never see that behavior again, that's a huge red flag.

We know of one great gal who has fallen into this trap. She has recently broken up with her boyfriend of three years, but she is still holding on to the hope that he "will come back to his senses." Their initial courtship was everything she ever dreamed about. They enjoyed long walks in the park, talking till the wee hours of the morning, and a strong physical attraction. Unfortunately, this phase lasted only about six months. It was followed by cheating, lying, and demonstrating a general disrespect of her as a woman. She hopes that somehow he will come back around and they will go back to what their relationship was like in the beginning. Big red flag: It was only six months out of a three-year relationship! The likelihood that they could ever get back to that point is slim. Oftentimes people just pretend to be who they think you want them to be. Eventually the mask comes off and what you see is what you get. Here is what she has to say about it:

I had hoped that our relationship would one day again be as great as it was in the beginning. I thought the relationship would change back to what it was like just as quickly as it had changed for the worse. I held on for a long time, but he didn't change back; he only slipped further away. I didn't want to let go of the future we had planned with each other. The picture was perfect. We had an idea of our dream wedding, our dream home, the perfect names for our children—but it was just a picture. It was and still is the future life I want. I care too much to let go.

It's great that she has a clear picture of what she wants out of her future life. However, it's never a good idea to force a guy into that picture. Especially one who doesn't want—or deserve—to be part of your future.

Settling: "All of the good guys are taken, and I am afraid no one better will come along."
Are you psychic? You cannot possibly know the outcome to this scenario. One thing is for sure, though: You will eliminate the opportunity to meet the right guy if you choose to stay with the wrong one. It's not just about finding a perfect guy. It's about finding the perfect guy for *you*. It is going to require you to do some work. Don't want a boyfriend who drinks too much and smokes? Then stop hanging out at bars waiting for someone to come up and talk to you. Evaluate what you want in a relationship. Once you do, take action. Action might be joining an online dating service, attending a singles event at your local church, volunteering at a soup kitchen, training for a half marathon. Be proactive. And don't expect the first guy

you meet to be the *one*. Take your time and do it right this time. Even after all of this hard work, you still may not find the right guy—but at least you will have your self-respect. And who knows what new friends you might meet along the way? You might even create a whole new network of single friends, which will remove another objection we heard: "All my friends are married."

It seemed that all of my friends were either married or in relationships. I had no idea how to meet single people my age. I became interested in yoga and found a class in one of the trendier parts of the city. I did not meet the man of my dreams in the class, but I did meet a few single gals who have become two of my closest friends. It's refreshing to be connected with people who are in the same relationship boat as I am. And they have a whole network of friends that I am now a part of.

Divorce: "If it doesn't work out I can always get divorced."
Far too many women have thrown this objection our way. We think this is pretty twisted logic! Every woman we interviewed who knew they were making a mistake as they walked down the aisle eventually went through a divorce. For some it took only six months, and for others it took twenty-five years. But *each and every one of them* spoke about their divorces as one of the most painful experiences of their lives. The women felt like failures and suffered emotional pain even when *they* were the ones to initiate the divorce. We tend to believe that the spouse who walks away from the marriage suffers no ill effects. That's simply not true. Too many women convince themselves to go ahead with mistaken marriages by

using divorce as their escape route. They say, "I'll just get a divorce if it doesn't work out." What they don't realize is that a divorce isn't that easy—even when you're the one who serves the papers.

That little voice kept saying, "You can just get married; you can always get divorced later." At that time, I was working in a small law firm and became close friends with the attorney's wife. We talked a lot about how I did not feel 100 percent sure of my relationship, and she told me that when she was younger, she, too, had called off her first engagement. It helped to see someone have that much courage. She helped me realize that I did not have to get married; it was my personal choice.

Don't fool yourself. Divorce is painful. It's painful for the husband, it's painful for the wife, and it's painful for the children. Divorce affects everyone around you.

✦   ✦   ✦   ✦

Jen's Story: An Adult Child of Divorce

Looking back at my early childhood, I can recall many good memories of my family. We had wonderful family traditions. Like all good Irish families, we treated St. Patrick's Day like it was Christmas! However, underneath all of that was a serious crisis. My parents did not get along very well. My childhood was not traumatic by any means. There was laughter in the house, my parents supported me in all my activities, and there was never any doubt that I was loved. The problem was between the two of them. And it went unspoken for almost twenty-five years.

I remember the phone call asking me to come to my parents' house. "We need to talk to you." My father-in-law had recently died after a long battle with cancer, so my heart sank, thinking I was going to have to find the courage to go through a similar situation with one of my own parents. The news was even more shocking and heartbreaking. My parents announced that they were separating. I felt like I had been hit over the head with a skillet, only it did not knock me out. I almost wish it had because I just sort of shut down at that point. My mom was crying, I could tell she was angry and hurt. My dad was also upset and tearful. He started to talk about how he had not been happy for almost sixteen years, and that he was no longer in love with my mom. I can't tell you exactly what the words were; there was a loud buzzing in my ear that kept me from fully hearing what was being said.

I was twenty-four years old, newly married, and in graduate school. I was having the time of my life, but it seemed to all disappear in that one moment. The reality of everything I thought I knew no longer existed. The safety and security I felt in my family, in the home they had created for us, felt insecure and completely annihilated. I asked my dad why he had waited so long to say something. Sixteen years is a long time to be living a lie. He said that he had hoped it would change or get better, but it never did. Once my brother and I had grown up and moved out there did not seem to be anything else to hold them together.

Their divorce was not cordial. To this day my parents have not spoken more than a few words to each other, much less been in the same room together. That part is frustrating. How do you live a life with someone for twenty-five years and then never speak to them again? My parents were alive and well; they did not die, but I was grieving in a way that I had never experienced before or since. As their marriage became dismantled, so did our whole family.

I have had the past thirteen years to take inventory of my parents' relationship. As much as it hurts, here is the reality:

- My parents barely knew each other when they got married. They had a long-distance courtship while my dad served in Vietnam. It may sound romantic, but that early romance did not last.

- My mom had doubts about her relationship with my dad on her wedding day. Parts of her story are sprinkled throughout this book.

- My parents fought with each other quite a bit. There was a lot of anger in those fights, and I never saw them apologize to each other.

- My dad drank a lot on the weekends, probably as a way to cope with his unhappiness. My mom hated his drinking. The more she criticized him the more he drank.

- My parents were judgmental and did not respect each other's differences.

- My parents rarely had dates together.

- They differed on their religious beliefs.

- They often disagreed on parenting styles and would argue about this in front of me and my brother.

- I do recall brief moments of their being happy together, but there are not many examples.

Although I am now much older, wiser, and more self-aware, the pain that I felt that day in my parents' living room will forever be with me. I still have a difficult time driving by the house where I grew up. The people who bought it have not taken care of it the way we did. The beautiful gardens my mom planted have become overgrown with weeds, and the new owners have put a huge privacy fence around the backyard. That house has become a symbol of how my family fell apart. I went through a roller coaster of emotions following my parents' separation and divorce. At the peak of the hill there was anger, then sadness, then guilt (I felt responsible in some ways for not being able to keep them together).

My parents' divorce is by far the most difficult thing I have ever dealt with and continue to deal with. I often wonder what the experience would have been like if I'd been a child. Going back and forth, splitting up holidays between two houses, not having the same financial resources. How would I have dealt with this as a child? I know as a grown, married adult, it was still upsetting. I don't blame my parents for the choices they made. They gave me life and I am grateful for that choice! I know I was conceived out of love, and I know that my parents love me—and I've never felt otherwise. I share my story with you not for pity, but to make you aware of the serious consequences of your actions. Getting married impacts everyone around you, and the consequences of divorce impact everyone around you, including your family, your friends, your children, your coworkers, your neighbors, and even your pets. That's why it's so important to remember that you can deal with all of this mess down the road, or you can simply walk away now, while there's time.

✦

Financial fears: "I can't financially support myself on my own."

We know this is a tough one. It's scary to think about making ends meet without a double income coming in. But think this through carefully, and try not to get too overwhelmed. We followed up with one of our now-divorced brides who thought it was going to be impossible to make it financially on her own. She walked away from a dream house in the country and the financial supplements from her husband's very wealthy parents. This financial security, however, came at too high of a cost.

I desperately wanted out of this marriage. I wanted to just be done with him, but it was not that simple. We had to split everything, and I gave in to many of his demands simply because I did not want him to slow down the divorce process. I guess some people would view that as giving in, but I honestly did not care who got to keep the washer and dryer. He wanted to keep the house, as it was on his parents' property. They paid for most of it, and I got back the little amount I gave him to renovate. It was not a lot of money, but it was mine. I had no idea how I was going to pay for a new life on my own. I literally went from living with my parents to living with him, but I was determined to do it.

My sister and brother-in-law offered to let me move into their basement. Not exactly the living arrangements I had dreamed of, but I knew it would be temporary until I could save up some more money. I lived with them for a year and took a second job as a tutor in the evenings and on weekends. I put myself on a tight budget and avoided debt. If I wanted to buy something, I did not get it unless I could pay with cash. I did this for a year, and I am pleased to say that I just moved into a cute little house that is all mine! Moving day was one of my proudest moments. It's not the Taj Mahal, but it is my own little palace. I don't wear designer clothes or have a luxury car like I did when I was married, but none of those "things" matter to me anymore. What matters is the self-respect I now have for myself and the reassurance that I really can make it on my own.

✦   ✦   ✦   ✦

How to Marry a Serial Husband

* Ignore the fact that you are his fourth fiancé.
* Believe him when he tells you that all of his ex-wives are crazy.

That way, when it's your turn to be his ex-wife, you'll finally understand why he had been married three times!

✦

First Comes Love, Then Comes Marriage . . .

How many of us sang this song while jumping rope on the playground? From that early age, it was ingrained in our little heads that a successful girl meets a boy, falls in love with the boy, marries the boy, then has babies with the boy, in that order! If you are reading this book, chances are that you are between the ages of eighteen and twenty-nine, the prime of youth. You have had at least one serious relationship by now, maybe even more than one. In the back of your head, that earlier message repeats over and over again and is almost impossible to tune out. By society's standards, if you are one of the unlucky women who cannot make this dream come true, then surely there is something wrong with you. The only way you can make your dreams come true is to get married.

Myth: Marriage = Instant Success and Happiness

Will the act of marrying *really* make you happy? Will it set you on the path to happiness? Is it a mark of success and achievement? In her book *The Starter Marriage and the Future of Matrimony,* author Pamela Paul talks about the statement that being married makes to others:

> Getting married sends a strong signal: You've got it all together. You're in control, on top of things. Being married creates a powerful message about who you are and where you're going, because we assume that once you're wed, the rest falls into place—the beautiful home, the gourmet dinner parties attended by other witty, vivacious couples, the glorious pregnancy— with a trouble-free healthy baby its proud result, the child-rearing years complete with nanny and perhaps some part-time work for Mom, comfortably carried out from her home office. The kids who always do their homework and get into prestigious schools, the fabulous family vacations to Tahoe and Paris and the Grand Canyon, and ultimately, home fires burning

into the golden years, furnished with grinning grand-
children and oversized family portraits. All you need
to do is marry; the attendant rewards are waiting.*

That sounds a little ridiculous, doesn't it? We know that
Paul has her tongue planted firmly in her cheek. But there is
some truth in the jest. Marriage often *is* idealized by our society. It also confirms your desirability: "Look! Someone
wanted to marry me, so I must be worthwhile." It's easy to
fall prey to this myth. And it is just that: *a big myth!*

Settling for a Ho-hum Relationship

By now you have taken a look at the red flags in your current
and past relationships. You have a bit of an understanding of
your gut feelings. You have acknowledged the objections that
keep you from breaking it off, but you just aren't sure what to
do. Take your time. There is no rush. Let's hear from two
more women who settled for ho-hum relationships:

*Even if things aren't right, it's difficult to make the big decision
to break up. Everyone is afraid of being alone. The relationship
is what you know, what's comfortable, and what you're used to
in your life. Getting out of that relationship makes things like
the weekend and hanging out with other couples stressful, because it's not normally something you have to plan or think
about when you're in a relationship.*

*Pamela Paul, *The Starter Marriage and the Future of Matrimony* (New
York: Villard Books, 2002), 42–43.

Even though it was wrong, I stayed. It was comfortable. I knew him, he knew me . . . we knew more about each other and understood each other better than anyone else. That didn't mean it would work, it just meant that I was settled and content at the time. We eventually split, for good reason. But I'd be lying if I said I don't miss the comfort level I had with him.

Don't think we are giving you permission to settle here. Remember—every woman we spoke to agreed to share her story in order to spare you from making the same painful mistake she did. They all suffered a great deal in order to get to a place of contentment with themselves. Listen and learn. They all agreed that if they had it to do over again, they never would have settled in their relationships. By doing so, they lost sight of themselves. What can you do to make sure you maintain your sense of self while remaining open to the possibility of having a healthy relationship with the right guy? Here's how one woman learned to truly value herself:

Single and Fabulous

Society often perceives being single as a curse, and I can tell you that it does have a dark side. But like everything in our world, it also has a light side. I love that I have had this time to get to know myself. Being single allowed me to do the inner work (or shall I say "undo" the misguided learnings from my earlier years!) to get to this place. It took me a while to understand and define who I am and who I am becoming. Being single allowed me to travel that journey consciously. That is the truest gift that being single has given to me. I also enjoy that I am able to have so many rich experiences in my life. As a single woman, if I want to make some-

thing happen, it is my choice to do that. I've learned a great deal about how I choose to handle my time, my money, and my choices.

Being single has strengthened me. . . . The opportunity to get to know who I truly am has strengthened me as a person. I was always a late bloomer, and had I married before I was ready, I would have been the wrong girl with the wrong guy.

For various reasons, I missed out on the experience of exploring dating and relationships in high school. I really didn't start dating until college, and my emotional age was still thirteen or fourteen. This led to a string of poor choices in dating partners—choices that only spiraled downward through my twenties and thirties.

By the time I hit my midthirties, the situation had finally called forth in me some deep soul-searching. I had to take a good look at the quality of my choices regarding relationships during the "prime" dating years of my life. It wasn't a pretty picture. And inside of me was the only place to go to make things better.

It's been several years since I've had a long-term relationship, and I can now say, without a shadow of a doubt, that I am a different woman today than I was back then. I like the woman I am today much better. She's smarter, more sure of herself, and owns what I like to call "the good, the bad, and the ugly" parts of her life. It took a long time to get to this point.

I feel I have not settled for less than the right marriage for me. I have always valued marriage deeply, and I still intend to create one.

Now that I've done the work and have gotten to know myself, the reasons that I want to join with the right guy to create a strong marriage are far more authentic.

Wise advice from a woman who has learned from her mistakes. The single life is not a curse. It's an opportunity for you to define who you are, search for what you want, and map out your own course.

Standing Alone to Make Good Choices for Your Life

In their book *The Good Marriage: How and Why Love Lasts,* Judith Wallerstein and Sandra Blakeslee talk about what is necessary to make a wise choice in marriage. They call it the ability to "stand alone":

> To stand alone, you must feel that you have a choice and that you merit a choice, that somebody will choose you and that you will have the opportunity to choose in return. Standing alone does not just mean living in your own apartment after college. It does mean being able to get through the night by yourself. It means not being driven by loneliness to make bad decisions about who you invite into your apartment. In my experience, many wretched marriages have resulted from the fear of being alone, even briefly.*

Do You Have the Ability to Stand Alone?
Ask yourself the following:
- Are you able to stand alone or are you held back by fear?
- What fears are keeping you in the wrong relationship?

---

*Judith S. Wallerstein and Sandra Blakeslee, *The Good Marriage: How and Why Love Lasts* (New York: Warner Books, 1995), 101.

• Are you making bad decisions about your relationships because you don't want to be alone? Why don't you want to be alone?

• Are you limiting yourself by remaining in a relationship that does not feel right to you?

• Which of these objections resonates with you?

"I wanted to have kids before the age of thirty. If I break up with him, I might not have a chance to have children because I will be too old."

"I don't want to hurt him. He needs me."

"He is going to change. He was so great when we started dating; I know that person is still inside of him."

"All of the good guys are taken, and I am afraid no one better will come along."

"If it doesn't work out I can always get divorced."

"I can't financially support myself on my own."

You must resist the urge to fall back on these objections. Don't believe that you are better off with the wrong guy rather than being alone. Plant your feet firmly on the ground and tell yourself, "I can stand alone! I am ready to make good choices in my life!" Now let's put those choices into action.

In the next chapter we will show you how to find the wisdom and courage to call off your relationship and/or engagement. Remember, by calling it off with the wrong guy, you open yourself up to the possibility of finding the right guy.

◆ 8 ◆

Just Say *No*
Calling It Off and Moving On

When in doubt, don't.

—Benjamin Franklin

No Easy Decision

The decision to end a relationship is not an easy one. It can be one of the most pivotal decisions of your life. But trust us when we tell you that you will be OK. You will survive this. There is a much better life waiting for you. Are you ready to move on?

Here, a woman who has had almost thirty years to reflect on her mistaken marriage speaks to you like a good friend:

Please understand that there are always other options. Yes, you might be hurting someone or closing some doors, but realize that hurting yourself *instead is rarely the right answer in life. People who truly love you wouldn't want you to be hurt at their expense. People who don't love in the ways that you need to be loved definitely aren't worth the sacrifice! Listen to your heart. If it's uncertain and confused and even a little scared, then just announce*

(DO NOT ASK) that you're taking some time out to think through things. You're sorry for the pain and stress that this might cause others (with wedding plans, money, reservations, and so on), but you need to take care of yourself. Those who love you will understand. Those who don't can go look in the mirror for a while and tell themselves how mean you are to put them through this. That's their problem, not yours. And if they react that way, then you have further reinforcement for not being a part of their lives.

The guilt trips that people can lay on you are incredibly hard to take sometimes. Be strong. Decisions like this are difficult and rarely clear-cut. Listen to your heart. Your caring side, the side that has been socialized since birth to take care of others at your expense, will tell you that maybe it won't be so bad, maybe he'll change, maybe once you get away from here, maybe, maybe, maybe you could learn to tolerate X, Y, or Z. The tiny little voice in your head that is learning to speak learns only through situations like this. It's not very strong yet, but it's telling you that you're disappointing the main stakeholder—which is you. You're selling yourself out in order to make someone else happy. Please don't do it. Your ability to be a happy, creative member of society and make this world a better place depends on it. Take care of yourself. You are a precious gift to the world, and your ability to explore those gifts to their fullest depends on your taking care of number one: you!

A Subject No One Likes to Talk About

No one likes to talk about canceled weddings. We called wedding planners, florists, caterers, and photographers to discuss their experiences. While they were pleasant, the minute we raised the issue of canceled weddings, we often heard a sharp intake of breath, or their voices dropped to a whisper. "Oh, yes, that does happen *sometimes*," they said, almost as if they didn't want to be associated with such unpleasantness. Our personal favorite response was "That doesn't really happen to us." Their attitude was that they were not the type of florist that would do business with someone who would cancel a wedding! When probed further, they admitted that it does happen, but apparently they were concerned that just talking about it might stir up some bad luck.

We spoke with one prominent catering executive whose company has a long history of handling the grandest events in his large Midwestern city.

If you are talking about weddings that are canceled in the time frame of seven to fourteen days before the scheduled date, I would say that we have experienced that only about ten times over the last twenty years. However, if you are talking about weddings that are canceled further in advance, say three to four months, I would say that number is about 10 percent.

We asked him about the logistics of canceling.

We require a 50 percent nonrefundable deposit to reserve the date. So if you cancel after you have paid your deposit, we do not refund the money. Usually it is the father of the bride who calls to cancel. Most of the time, people realize that it is cheaper to go forward and have a party anyway, since they have already spent the money. That seems to be the trend lately. . . . They go ahead and celebrate, even though it is no longer a wedding reception.

With his many years' experience catering weddings, we asked whether it was obvious when a couple's wedding was a mistake.

Yes, absolutely. There is no doubt in my mind. . . . It is written all over the face of the bride or groom. There is a difference between someone displaying the nerves associated with a big event versus someone who is just going through the motions. All of our staff can recognize this at a wedding reception. We also see it in the temperament of the bride or groom leading up to the event—when they are unpleasant or difficult to deal with. It's as if they take their frustration about their relationship and upcoming wedding out on those who are serving them. An angry bride or groom is usually an unhappy bride or groom.

The Ones Who Called It Off

The ones who called it off paid attention to those gut feelings we've been talking about. They also found the courage to take action and cancel their weddings. How did they do it? We asked everyone to look back and try to describe the event that triggered their decision to cancel—the straw that broke the camel's back, so to speak. Some people could not pinpoint a specific event; they just knew that it wasn't right and they couldn't go through with it. But most people were able to recall in very clear detail the moment they knew they had to call it off.

My fiancé and I had bought a new home together and decided to live together for one year before our wedding. He made a good living, so we ended up purchasing a 3,300-square-foot home. I thought I'd be happy no matter what. Who wouldn't be happy living in this beautiful new place with a guy who adored both my son and me? Wrong! Everything inside me screamed it was horribly wrong. I didn't love him—not the way a wife should love a husband. After the first week of living together I had what I describe as a nervous breakdown. Even though I was living in a large, beautiful home, I felt like I was caged in a tiny jail cell. I couldn't breathe. I couldn't eat. I couldn't sleep. I cried every day and screamed at everyone. I knew right then and there that I would not be able to stay with him a minute longer.

I knew I had to call it off when a close friend of ours passed away. When it happened, my fiancé was not supportive of my feelings. In fact, he refused to talk about the situation. For a while I convinced myself that it was a part of his grieving process that caused him to be so cold, but I soon realized that his actions were impacting my own grieving in a way that wasn't healthy for me. This made me realize that his priorities were himself and his work—period.

I called my wedding off approximately three weeks before the big day. I had gone out with the girls for my bachelorette party, and by the time I came home, the sun was about to come up. Needless to say, I had had entirely too much to drink and barely remembered my own name, let alone the events of the evening. As I came into the home we shared, my fiancé began to question me about where I had been and who I had been sleeping with, and so on and so forth. It seemed like a never-ending cycle of being hounded about my actions. (This wasn't the first time. He was always questioning my whereabouts. I couldn't go anywhere without him thinking I was cheating on him.) Finally after a few hours of the interrogation, I went to sleep and woke up the next morning (which was Easter morning), and I called my mom and told her I would be coming home. My mom said, "Oh, for Easter dinner?" I said, "No, forever." I told her that I could not live my life this way any longer. I could not imagine being hounded every day of my life. If it was this bad before we were married, imagine what it would be like in ten years.

My final straw wasn't really some big, momentous event. It evolved over a few months. The wedding was nearing and I left the country to do some modeling in Japan and make more money to pay for the big day. When I was finally out from under his thumb, I realized how much I had going for me and that I didn't need him to supply my self-esteem. I became more independent and began to see how he had been manipulating me into becoming a more submissive woman. He was controlling and it took getting away from him to see it. The more times I talked about him, or wrote in my journal about us, the easier it was for me to see our relationship the way it really was. I felt stronger and more empowered to assert myself, and I realized that I had been afraid of him for so many reasons. It may seem like I "chickened out" by calling off our wedding from the other side of the world, but it was the smartest thing I could have done. He was unable to coerce me or threaten me or try to convince me that I needed him to be loved or successful. I really felt strong, capable, and independent away from him. My instincts to call it off from afar proved to be right!

What can we learn from these stories? Not one single woman who canceled her wedding regretted it. They only regretted not doing it sooner!

✦   ✦   ✦   ✦

The Break-up Conversation

If telling your family seems difficult, telling your fiancé is even harder. It *will* be a difficult conversation. While the pain may be with both of you for a while, the conversation does not need to go on for hours. Think about what you want to say beforehand. Talk to someone you trust before you do it to help you choose your words carefully. Remember, the truth hurts, but the truth will free you from a really awful mistake.

✦

On Courage

There is so much pressure on the bride-to-be—it's hard to stop that wedding train once it's barreling down the tracks. We asked our brave panel why they think they had the courage to act.

I believe that part of the reason I was able to act on my instincts to call it off was because I spent time away from him, on my own. Reflecting, journaling, making new friends, having fun, and feeling like I was OK on my own were so important. I was out from under his choke hold, and it felt good. I think taking some time and space for me *was the key to tapping into my inner courage.*

Prayer gave me the courage! God helped me out of that mess—there's no way I could have done it on my own.

I think my courage came from the strong sense that this decision was bigger than me—the sense that, in some ways, I really didn't have a choice. I felt so deeply that it would be a disaster to follow through with it.

I think my courage came from understanding and knowing who "I" was separate from who "we" were. It took me a long time to find that, but once I did, I rediscovered what I deserve in a relationship. Also, knowing that my family and friends wanted me to be happy—over anything else—was a huge help for me.

Think about the real reasons you are getting married. Is it because all your friends are getting married and you want to fit in? Are you afraid if you don't marry this guy you might not find anyone else? Do you think you need a husband for security? Don't sell yourself short. *I didn't get married until I was thirty-nine years old, and my husband was forty-four. Neither one of us had been married before! We have a beautiful daughter, a great life, and a wonderful marriage. Good things do come to those who have the courage and wisdom to wait!*

I rely on my religious faith. That's why I recommend that you pray very deeply for God to guide you, and pay attention to how you are feeling. When it's right, it is easy and natural, and now that I'm happily married, I am witness to that. It really was through constant prayer and focus on marriage as a sacrament that helped me see things progressively more clearly as the day approached, so that I could call it off with confidence and peace

one month before. I put my trust in God, not worldly things,
and it turned out so much better than I could have imagined.

You Can Do It, Too!

So there you have it. These women demonstrated great
courage. But they didn't have to jump out of an airplane or
scale Mount Everest. They simply responded to their inner
wisdom and acted on it. And they had no regrets—not a single one. We never regret doing the right thing. Yes, it may be
painful or embarrassing in the short term, but it's the right
decision in the long term. Just ask the women who didn't call
it off! They'll set you straight. In fact, they will do just about
anything to keep you from following them down the aisle.
Ask yourself:

• Do I have the courage to do the right thing? (Answer:
Yes. If your answer is no, reread the preceding words of wisdom from those who called it off.)

• If I don't take action now, what will I regret? Getting
married to the wrong person? Staying in an unsatisfying relationship?

• What words of wisdom resonated with me? Can I see
myself in these stories?

Be completely honest as you ask yourself these tough questions. You are getting closer to making that pivotal decision.

What's It Like to Call It Off?

Yes, it takes courage and wisdom to call off your wedding or
end your relationship. You know what the red flags are. You

are paying attention to your gut feelings. Now your head is spinning, and you don't know where to begin. Take a deep breath and consider the following steps:

> **Step 1. Give yourself some time to just think about calling it off.**
>
> **Step 2. Say the words out loud: "I want to call it off."**
>
> **Step 3. Take action: The secret is to do *something*!**

Step 1: Give yourself some time to just think about calling it off.

It is easy to get overwhelmed by the thought of this monumental task. There are too many people to tell, the showers have been scheduled, the flowers have been ordered, and the towels have already been monogrammed. Rather than getting lost in all of the party-planning details, Try this:

• Think about what it would be like to tell just one person about your doubts and fears about your pending marriage. Maybe that person is your mom or your best friend. How will they respond? How do you *want* them to respond? Why did you pick this particular person to tell? Is it because you know they will support you unconditionally? The answers to these questions will give you a clue about what you really want to do and what you want to hear.

• How do you think you'll feel after you tell that first person that you want to call off your wedding? Many women told us that they felt like a huge weight was lifted off their shoulders after they called off their weddings. Picture it in your own mind. Can you imagine a huge weight being lifted from your shoulders? Maybe you can visualize it as thousands of balloons being released to the sky. Whatever imagery works for you, it is important to picture yourself taking that first step. You might be surprised by how freeing this decision will be.

• Don't try to talk yourself out of what you are feeling. It is important to stop and pay attention. Don't dismiss any reservations you are feeling as "just jitters." Instead, carefully examine your feelings, fears, and concerns.

Simply giving thought to your feelings, fears, and concerns may be all it takes to put you on the right path to self-discovery. You don't have to call off the wedding this very minute. You don't need to dump your boyfriend right now. You simply need to start the process of uncovering the stressors related to your current relationship or pending marriage. Once you do this, you may discover how courageous you can be! Remember, the long-term costs of a bad marriage far outweigh the short-term embarrassment or financial cost of a canceled wedding. Need proof? Go through this book for clues on what you have to look forward to if you marry the wrong man. You might end up like these women:

We got in a fight on the second night of our honeymoon because he ran into people he knew and he wanted to have dinner with them. They were strangers to me and I wanted him to myself. He didn't care.

I realized I had really made a mistake the day after our wedding, on our European honeymoon. We needed a little time to "come down" from all the excitement. There was just the two of us—no one else to reminisce with. We were jet-lagged. I caught a cold, got a yeast infection, and started my period all at the same time. We got in a horrible fight and were sniping at each other constantly. It was just fraught with emotion. It was very telling that the two of us could not get along on what was supposed to be a romantic honeymoon abroad.

Step 2: Saying the words out loud: "I want to call it off."

Admitting that your relationship is wrong is very difficult. Accepting it and acting on it is even harder. What role do other people play in this decision? Sharing deeply private information can be tricky, because you never know how other people will respond. You also run the risk that they will try to talk you out of doing what you know is right. For the most part, everyone we interviewed said that telling others about their decision was difficult but cathartic.

I think my mom always knew that I was not truly happy with my fiancé. It is that whole "mother's intuition." I think I was in that stage in my life where I just wanted to get married. My family was supportive. Of course, my parents lost some money on deposits that they were not too thrilled about, but they would rather have me call it off than get divorced a year later.

I told my parents and friends. Everyone was extremely supportive and relieved. It was as if everyone knew I was unhappy before I did. In the end, all they wanted for me was to be happy.

My parents and best friend knew I was calling it off before my fiancé did. My parents could see how upset I had been, so they were 100 percent supportive. Even though they loved my fiancé very much, they knew I had to break it off. My friends felt all along that I was making a mistake when I got engaged. I've always been a hopeless romantic. I loved being in love.

I called off the wedding exactly one month and one day before the date. I felt so strongly about calling it off that I don't think I weighed the consequences—it just didn't matter at all to me what people thought. In fact, I remember thinking after I did it that people might think I was a wimp or childish or afraid of moving (because I was going to move far away from home, to Dallas), but to my surprise, all these random girls (friends of friends of friends) called me to congratulate me on being so brave. It was so nice.

✦　✦　✦　✦

Anne's Story: "Guess what? It's a boy!" "That's great. I want to call off my wedding."

We were in the middle of a heat wave. As an unemployed gal, I was free to sit by the subdivision pool and read. Although I was looking for a job, I had a lot of unstructured time. (Oh, who am I kidding? Yes, I was looking for a job, but I was kind of halfhearted about it. Deep down I really didn't want to commit to a job in his hometown because I was feeling so conflicted about our relationship and upcoming marriage.) I would stake out a lounge chair in the back corner and watch all of the neighborhood moms and kids do their summertime thing. It was here where I began to think ahead to what my married life—right in this very neighborhood—was going to look like. And I didn't like what I saw.

First of all, my fiancé didn't like to spend time outside, and I did. I loved the heat, the sun, and swimming. There was a clubhouse adjacent to the pool with a playground and barbecue pits. The neighbors gathered here all summer long. I knew my fiancé wouldn't stick his big toe in the water and there would be no barbecuing for us. He wasn't much for socializing, either. I tried to imagine what kind of a dad he would be as I watched the kiddos splash in the water. It was sort of grim. We really hadn't even talked about our plans for a family. I had always hoped that I would have children, but when I thought about it, I couldn't see myself having children with him. In fact, the thought of being tied to him for life through a child was an unpleasant one. And yes, I was still engaged to him! What sort of logic was that? Looking back, it is really hard to believe that that woman by the pool was *me*! None of it makes any sense. Why would you be engaged to a person who, when pressed, you can't imagine having children with? Lucky for me, however, my inner voice would not be silenced. I just knew I could not marry him and had to do something—but what?

The day after my poolside revelation, my dear friend Kathleen called from a hospital in Dallas. Just one hour postpartum, she was bursting with the good news of her bouncing baby boy. And what did I say in response to her glad tidings? "I can't marry him," I whispered. "I'm going to leave him." In two brief sentences I managed to suck all the joy out of her announcement and drag her into my messy life. That's what friends are for! God love her—she instantly shifted gears and put on her "friend-counselor" hat. I can't remember exactly what she said, but the bottom line was that she supported me. She told me that I should do what I had to do. She told me exactly what I needed to hear. Her support set the wheels in motion for my departure. I don't know if I ever properly thanked her for that. In fact, I don't think I even sent a baby gift—I was too busy returning my wedding gifts.

✦

Are you surprised by how supportive the friends and family of these women were about their decisions to call it off? You shouldn't be. Everyone who knows and loves you has your best interests at heart. You need to trust them. Don't be afraid to admit to others that you are struggling with your decision to get married. You don't necessarily have to rent a billboard in Times Square to share your feelings, but you know who is safe to confide in. If you just don't have the support of friends and family then talk to a mentor, such as a religious adviser or spiritual director. If you are involved in your church, synagogue, or so forth, seek out direction from someone you trust. They most likely have been trained to deal with situations like yours, and if you can approach them without shame or guilt, they could be very helpful. You may also want to seek the guidance of a therapist.

A Few Words About Therapy

◆

*W*e found it curious that among all the women we talked to, only a few said they had turned to therapists to help sort out their reservations about their pending marriages.

Soon after moving in with him I began to have this gnawing feeling that something was wrong. I just didn't feel like he was in a joyful, happy place, and I sensed fear and anxiety from him. I suggested that we go see a therapist and talk about what was going on. It was during the counseling session that I realized for certain that this man did not want to marry me. Our wedding date was only two weeks away, and I was completely devastated. But I knew that calling off the wedding was the only thing to do.

The therapist was extremely instrumental in helping both of us. She helped him find the courage to be completely honest with me and tell me that he really didn't want to marry me, and she helped me come to the conclusion that calling off the wedding was the only choice.

She also told him he needed to do whatever I asked of him in regard to calling off the wedding and helping me get my life back together. I placed a lot of blame on him. From the beginning, I had been clear that I was not going to force him to marry me. I wanted him to be 100 percent sure. He had told me that he was certain, and then I had started planning everything: a wedding, a cross-country move, and a job change. This was all based on the belief that he was ready to marry me.

The therapist had known the gist of the problem before we even walked in the door. I had spoken with her on the phone that morning, and she met with us later that day. I think the whole session was less than two hours. The way she expedited my personal emergency was superb.

The therapist was very skilled. She spoke to the two of us together first. Then she asked me to leave the room, and she spoke to him by himself. Then she spoke to us together, and she asked him to explain to me what he had shared with her. He told me that he didn't want to get married. She then talked to me alone about what I wanted from him in order to get my life back, and she made some suggestions to me. After that, she spoke to the two of us together, and I shared with him what I needed from him. She asked him if these were reasonable requests, and he, of course, agreed to do whatever it would take.

We went to the therapist together only once. We decided to call off the wedding, and I flew home within days. I moved in with my mom and went to therapy on my own for probably five or six sessions. The new therapist helped me work through my grief and helped me focus on moving forward. I got very lucky and found a job within a couple of months of returning home. So anything is possible. Because I was able to secure a job, and with the money I had from the engagement ring, I moved out of my mom's house and bought my first house shortly thereafter.

I would highly recommend that anyone who is having doubts about getting married go and see a good therapist. If you think your fiancé is the one having doubts about getting married, then I recommend that you go together. The key is to get a really good counselor. Ask someone you know who is in the field, or ask someone you know who has actually seen a good one themselves.

Jennifer's Advice: Common Obstacles to Therapy and How to Find a Qualified Therapist

✦

It can be difficult to seek out a therapist and ask for help. There seems to be a certain amount of shame and/or fear surrounding therapy. But as you can see in the above situation, the counselor was instrumental in helping this couple decide to call off their wedding. Let's look at the most common myths versus facts regarding therapy:

Myth: Therapy is too expensive.

Fact: A good therapist today will typically charge $100 and up, depending on what part of the country you live in.

This charge is hourly; the typical therapy session lasts fifty minutes. However, do you really want to balk at this cost? You cannot put a price tag on your happiness.

If you spend just four or five sessions determining what you need to do regarding your relationship, life, and happiness, that will be money well spent!

Myth: Only the real "crazies" go into therapy, and I know I am not crazy.

Fact: Your mental well-being should be of the utmost importance to you.

Therapists do not work with just the severely mentally ill. In fact, many therapists agree that it's the healthiest, most balanced people who seek help for problems that are impacting their daily lives. If depression and anxiety are interfering with your sleeping and eating, it's important to get some help. Talking to a therapist can help you find solutions and get your life back in balance.

Myth: A total stranger will not be able to help me with my personal problems.

Fact: One of the greatest benefits of therapy is having a trained, professional "outsider" help you see the situation without bias and prejudice.

A good therapist (and yes, there *are* bad ones out there) will serve as a guide to help you navigate the rough and heavy terrain of your life and your relationship. They will help point out the pitfalls, hidden hazards, and road bumps that are hindering you from making the necessary changes in your life. A therapist cannot *make* you change; however, they can offer a safe place for you to discover what you need to do. A word of caution: If a therapist does claim to be able to *make* you change, it is time to find a different therapist.

If you decide to take a leap of faith and see a therapist, here are two important things to consider:

How do you find a good, qualified counselor?

Do your homework. Conduct some research. Check with your insurance company. They most likely will have a list of mental health providers that are in your network. It is a daunting task to try to pick someone from a list of hundreds. If you must select a therapist from a list, know that you will need to spend some time making the right choice. Talk to your primary care physician, your friends, and so on, and ask if they can recommend someone on the list. Then call each of the recommended therapists and try to get a sense of who they are over the phone. This is another example of trusting your gut! Not all therapists have a PhD in psychology; it simply means that they have a doctorate in their field of study. But if you prefer to see a therapist with a PhD, that is a good place to start winnowing your list. Other credentials to be aware of are LCSW (licensed clinical social worker), LPC (licensed professional counselor), and LMFT (licensed marriage and family therapist). The exact titles vary by state, and regardless of the initials behind their name, the key is that they are licensed. Every state has specific licensing guidelines that must be met every year. Most licensed professionals have at least a master's degree. It is *not* recommended that you see someone who claims to be a therapist but is not licensed to practice clinically. Life coaching is a new trend in the field of psychotherapy. If you choose to go this route, find out if the therapist is licensed as well. Some therapists who are already licensed in their fields are now calling themselves coaches.

Will my insurance pay for therapy?

Health care benefits are not what they used to be. Most insurance companies do offer some benefits for mental health, but they vary. If you have an HMO, you will have access only to the list of providers they give you. If you choose to go out of your network, you will have to cover the cost of therapy. If you have a PPO, you will have the choice of using a provider in or out of the network. If you use an out-of-network therapist, you will pay more of the cost. Your insurance company will determine how many sessions they will pay for, and it is often fewer than what you will actually need. Be proactive and find out what the specifics of your coverage are so that you are not surprised with a large invoice. You should also be aware that the insurance companies have access to your records, so if your privacy is something that you want to maintain, you might want to consider paying for your sessions out of pocket.

For more help on finding a counselor, please refer to the resource section at the end of this book.

Step 3: Take action: The secret is to do *something*!

We believe that there are more people who go through with mistaken marriages than those who call them off. Based on all of the research we have conducted, we believe that if you talk to ten divorced women, three of them knew it was a mistake as they were walking down the aisle. As you have just read, it is difficult to decide that you need to call off your wedding or end your relationship. Taking action on this knowledge is even harder. We believe everyone has the ability to hear their inner voices and act on their feelings—but something stops them. How can you tap into your courage and take action?

First, can you tell the difference between canceling a party and ending a relationship? The challenge is admitting that what you really want to do is end the relationship itself. Unfortunately, people get so caught up in the details surrounding the ceremony and reception that they feel they have to go through with it. They are paralyzed by the thought of telling their friends and family, the florist, and the caterer that the wedding is off. It seems silly when you look ahead. Will the caterer be there when your future husband is out drinking every night with his buddies? Will the florist help you out around the house when your husband refuses to do the laundry? Think of it this way: Your one and only task is to end the relationship. Your friends and loved ones can help you cancel the party.

Many women knew they should end the relationship itself—but the party got in the way. Ask yourself:

1. What is stopping me from calling off my wedding?

2. Is my hesitation related to any of the following issues?

- Money spent on the dress, flowers, shoes, reception
- A feeling that it is too late to cancel the big party—being caught up in the momentum
- Embarrassment over telling my wedding party that the party's off. (Quit picturing your friends in their taffeta bridesmaid dresses; they are your friends first!)
- Disappointing people who are excited about the wedding

These are all issues related to canceling a party. Don't let the party-planning issues muddy the waters.

Next, ask yourself:

3. Deep down, do I really want to end the entire relationship?

4. If the answer is yes, make a list of all the reasons why. Some examples:

- He is disrespectful to me. He has treated me poorly throughout the wedding planning process, and I know it will get worse after the wedding.
- I can see some major family problems brewing. His mother does not like me, and he does not support me. I have talked about it until I am blue in the face, and he will not acknowledge my concerns.
- He has a hard time keeping a job and always seems to blame others for his misfortune.

- He has a problem abusing alcohol, and he seems to be drinking more. He gets defensive when I talk about it.

We don't mean to be redundant, but, if we've said it once, we've said it a hundred times: *Problems will not get better after the wedding.* This woman cites practically every single one of the reasons listed above as to why she didn't call off her wedding. Wait until you see how her story ended.

As we moved ahead with our wedding plans, my fiancé voiced some minor doubts about getting married. We talked about it and then we moved on. This just escalated as the wedding got closer. Little by little he shared some information about a female coworker he had befriended, and he said he was having mixed feelings about getting married to me because of his feelings for her. I was confused and not sure what it all meant. He said he still wanted to be married to me, and we continued to plan the wedding.

As the wedding got closer, it was harder and harder to overlook the information he had shared about the other woman. I had kept it to myself for four months, but I finally got up the nerve to tell my family what was going on. I then learned some information about my fiancé and this woman that led me to believe they might be more than friends. He denied all of it and said she was just a neutral friend he could talk to about all the stresses in his life. I was so blinded by my white dress, cake, invitations, limo, and plans for the ceremony that I couldn't think straight. We went to counseling for a while and were encouraged to cancel the wedding. I didn't want to. I was devastated by the thought of not getting married and not marrying this man, who I thought I was in love with.

We looked into what it would cost to cancel all the vendors and to possibly postpone the wedding. We learned we would lose all the money, so we talked about it and decided not to cancel. I logically knew that he would not change. I also knew deep down that marriage would not improve the problems we had and, in fact, it would only make them permanent. Unfortunately, my heart was telling me that marriage was the commitment that he needed. He promised me he was going to be the husband that I always wanted. My family voiced some concerns, but overall they just wanted me to be happy, and I said I was. At the time, I honestly thought I was . . . or at least on the surface I was.

Ever since I was a little girl, I had wanted to be married and be a mom. He was the first boyfriend that I ever had who told me he wanted to marry me. I clung to that during our six-year relationship. I was scared to start over, and I thought that marriage meant the same to him. I thought that his having a wife was the commitment he needed to be loyal to me.

Honestly, I was so happy when I was walking down the aisle. It was a dream come true. I was in my church where I grew up with all my family and closest friends around me. I was in a beautiful dress and having the wedding I always wanted. I do remember feeling happy that my fiancé showed up. I was a little nervous about this prior to the day. . . .

During our engagement, my fiancé would not let me put our engagement announcement in the newspaper. He told me that I could put our wedding announcement in after the wedding. So about one month after we were married, I put our wedding photo and announcement in the local paper. He came home from work one day and was angry that I had done this, because his coworkers had apparently seen it and asked him about it. That's when I found out that no one at his workplace knew he had gotten married! He had never even told them he was engaged!

Things just got worse after that, and I kept catching him in lie after lie. We had planned to take our honeymoon four months after the wedding. We had our tickets purchased and were ready to go. About a week before our trip my now-husband got a text message that I read on his phone. It was at midnight from his "friend" from work. It read, "I miss you; I wish we were sleeping together." I was obviously furious and hurt. He denied doing anything with her and kept telling me that he did not understand why she would send that. When I wouldn't stop talking about it, he turned it around and blamed me for invading his privacy and looking at his phone. He then played the victim so that I would beg him for forgiveness. I was so torn about what to do. We had not even gone on our honeymoon, and I didn't know what to believe. He wouldn't admit anything.

After we both calmed down he said he thought it would be a good idea to go on the trip to get away and just concentrate on our relationship. This was a huge mistake. He was mean the entire week and didn't want to do anything with me. He told me on our honeymoon that he wanted a divorce and would go see a lawyer as soon as we got home. I was devastated. To me, marriage was forever, *but the day after we got home from our honeymoon, I moved out. The marriage had lasted barely four months.*

If you are having any doubts at all about getting married, do not do it. Life is too short to be unhappy. If it is meant to be, then it will happen. You must take a step back to figure out your thoughts. I would highly recommend premarital counseling. Stick with it until you work through all of your issues to make sure you are doing the right thing. Often there are so many things pulling at you, such as family, friends, coworkers, the wedding plans, future life plans, and so on, that it is hard to work through what you really want. Talking to a neutral party can really help you figure that out. Don't marry if you are not sure. It will just be harder later if you realize it after the wedding.

✦   ✦   ✦   ✦

How to Marry a Lazy Pothead

- Look the other way when he exhibits a poor work ethic.
- Ignore the smell of weed in his car.
- Do not add up the money he spends on his pot habit.
- Pay no attention to the hours he spends playing video games.

That way, you'll be sure to end up like this woman:

After our wedding, he was in a lot of debt and I helped him get out of it. He was a foreman on a construction crew. He stayed in the same job; he had no ambition. He was constantly smoking pot. I wanted to help fix his problems. After two years, I finally got hit by a bolt of lightning. I realized that he had cut off all his friendships and was playing video games constantly. He had no independent activities. He was self-medicating and withdrawing into himself; he was constantly stoned. He got on Prozac. It was either rage or nothingness.

✦

How to Tell Your Friend She Is Dating the Wrong Guy

We can't go anywhere without someone asking us, "How can I tell my friend-daughter-sister-niece-cousin she is dating the wrong guy?" We recently received an email from a woman who was panicked about her sister's upcoming wedding.

My sister Katie has lost her mind! She's engaged to a total loser and is about to make the biggest mistake of her life. She's a brilliant researcher, a talented musician, and a wonderful friend. Her fiancé is out of work and has no ambition. Katie does everything for him. She cooks, she cleans, and she pays his bills while he sits around playing video games all day. I have shared my concerns, but she says she loves him and that I simply don't understand what a great guy he is.

Katie's response is typical. Women put their blinders on when it comes to men and shut out their friends' comments and concerns. Here's what a few young women said about conversations they had (or didn't have) with friends who were with men who were all wrong:

I have said something to one girl, but she didn't even listen. When she found out that our friends were right, she felt bad. I've learned not to speak up if they're in too deep, because they won't listen anyway.

I have said things to the point where we aren't friends anymore, but she won't listen to me. She thinks what they have is perfect and won't listen to anyone else no matter what people say. I guess love is really, really, really blind. I have another friend who is with the wrong guy right now, but I haven't said anything to her after seeing what it has done to my other friendship. I don't want the same thing to happen with her, so I'm keeping my mouth shut. If I said anything to her it wouldn't change anything between the two of them, so I don't want to say something and risk our friendship.

This boy kept cheating on my friend, and when they would break up I would be there for her to comfort her and to let her vent. But then she would keep going back to him and keep going back to him, so finally I gave up trying to help, because I knew that anything I said or anything I did wasn't going to make a difference.

A friend of mine was getting married and the groom was a snake, asking each of the bridesmaids out. After the bridesmaids compared notes, I was the only one strong enough to tell the bride about it. She, of course, took his side and vowed we would never speak again.

Unfortunately, most women feel that they shouldn't speak up. They've been burned when they tried to help before, and they don't want to get burned again. We disagree. You must say something. You owe it to your friend or loved one.

Speak Up!

We are a community of women, and we need to be real and honest with one another. If you are a mother concerned about your daughter, the same is true for you. If you saw your daughter trapped in a speeding car headed for a cliff, would you stand by and watch, hoping and praying things would work out for her? Of course not! Think of her relationship as that speeding car. You must do everything within your power to stop her from crashing. Whether you are a friend or a relative, here are your options:

Option 1: Don't say anything.
Result: You now have a not-so-real friendship because you have to pretend to be supportive of her choice in a husband. You make excuses for not wanting to spend time with them because he makes your skin crawl. You slowly drift apart, and the very thing you were trying to avoid (losing her as a friend) happens anyway.

Option 2: Tell her your concerns in a caring and compassionate way. (Details on how to do this follow.)
What do you have to lose? Your friendship has already been impacted; just look at Option 1. Give her a little bit of credit, too. Don't just assume she is going to drop you if you share how you really feel. What if it actually has the opposite effect? What if she were desperately waiting for someone to give her permission to call it off?

This woman *wished* her friends had said something:

I wish my friends would have said something to me. I know they didn't want to hurt my feelings and were afraid to tell me what they really thought. I'm sure I would have been defensive about it, but deep down I knew he was all wrong for me. Their concerns might have helped me tap into the courage I needed to get out of that misguided relationship.

Here's how to have that difficult conversation. By approaching the conversation in this way, you might have a better chance of actually being heard.

Five Things You Can Do to Help Her See the Light
1. Speak up.
2. Validate, then activate.
3. Be nonjudgmental.
4. Shift the focus to you by using "I" statements.
5. Offer concrete help.

1. Speak up.
What do you have to lose? There is a good chance your friend will ignore you (or, even worse, end your friendship), but you owe it to her to say something. Yes, she might get defensive, or it may damage your friendship. But think about it this way—if she *does* end up marrying the wrong guy, your friendship will most likely be impacted anyway. Who wants to hang out with an unemployed video game addict?

2. Validate, then activate.
It's easier to see the truth from a position of strength rather than weakness. Start off by pointing out some of her best qualities. For example, "I have always admired your compassion for others; you deserve to be treated the same way." Start with a compliment, and she may be more receptive to what you are telling her.

3. Be nonjudgmental.

You understand your friend's strengths and weaknesses. Avoid pushing her buttons. Try to sit down with her and share your concerns in a way that does not come across as judgmental. Don't say, "We can't believe you are going to throw your life away by marrying this idiot." Instead, you can say, "It's difficult for me to be honest with you because I am afraid it might damage our friendship." This may give her permission to be honest with herself and open the door for further communication.

4. Shift the focus to you by using "I" statements.

We use this approach a lot in therapy, and it is a wonderful tool for defusing difficult conversations. Frame your concerns by starting with "I." For example: "I feel so uncomfortable when he puts you down and calls you names." Or say, "I really worry about how isolated you have become since you got engaged to him." She is much less likely to become defensive with this approach than if you tell her, "You are dating a jackass!"

5. Offer concrete help.

Help your friend by eliminating any excuses she has for not ending the relationship. For example, if she is living with her boyfriend, invite her to stay with you for a few days. Tell her you will help her find a new place, and call in the troops to help her pack and move. If wedding plans are under way, tell her that you will cancel the party—and she can cancel the relationship. Say, "I will call all the vendors and try to get your deposits back, plus, I'll work with your family to take care of the rest of the wedding details." Lifting these practical burdens may be all she needs to send her boyfriend packing.

How to Listen When Your Friends Express Concerns About *Your* Relationship

We are not going to let you off the hook yet. What about your own relationships? If you can dish it out, you have to be able to take it, too. What if *you* are the one dating the wrong guy? Sometimes the truth hurts.

I was going to be his fourth wife. My grandfather said to me, "Three women cannot be wrong!" I wish I would have paid attention!

Two of my friends tried to intervene and tell me not to marry him. He turned it around on them—as if they were the problem. It ruined my friendships. We didn't talk again until years later, after I divorced. No one else tried to say anything after what happened with those two friends.

My friends couldn't stand him. They couldn't understand why I was with him. They used to say he had a personality like a doorknob. My friends would see him out with other girls and tell me he was cheating on me. Of course, he always had an answer when I confronted him about this.

These women wish they had listened to their friends. Why didn't they? We've talked about the most common reasons women stay with the wrong guys. They are desperately afraid of being alone, and that fear drives them to make the wrong decision. What's behind your decision to ignore your friends?

Are You Not Listening?

Are you ignoring your friends' and family's suggestions that your boyfriend might not be the right person for you? Their warnings are red flags! Hindsight is 20/20. Put on your glasses and take a good, hard look at your relationship now. Replay those conversations you have had with others about your relationship or upcoming nuptials.

- What kind of body language does your best friend have when you talk about your boyfriend?
- How many of your friends are not coming to your wedding?
- What messages—verbal and nonverbal—are you receiving from others?

Deep down, you know the answer. Why would your friends risk posing these questions to you? They are not jealous, upset, or vengeful. It is not that they don't understand what a difficult childhood, home life, or amount of stress your boyfriend is enduring. Here's the thing: A difficult childhood, home life, or stress does not give you a free pass for being a jerk. There are millions of people in the world who were dealt a bad hand in life, and yet they still went on to be decent human beings. Stop making excuses for him. By turning a deaf ear, you are denying yourself true happiness. You need to listen.

Become an Active Listener

If you find yourself on the receiving end of this conversation, there are a few things you can do to ensure that you understand what your friends and family are trying to say.

1. Take off the boxing gloves.

Your initial response to this conversation may be to defend yourself and your boyfriend. No one is attacking you or him. They are simply concerned about you and want you to be open to what they have to say.

2. Check in with your fears.

Is your fear of being alone preventing you from hearing what is being said? Fear can be a powerful emotion. If at all possible, try to turn down the fear volume.

3. Consider what your friend is saying.

Have you been holding back from making a decision to leave your boyfriend because the process of breaking up is too overwhelming? She is here to help. Don't be afraid to ask her for what you need.

We have spoken to countless women who said, "My friends tried to warn me, but I just didn't listen." Unless you surround yourself with a school of piranhas, your friends and family are probably looking out for your best interests. *Listen, listen, listen* not only to your inner voice but to the voices of the people who care about you most. If more than one friend or relative has expressed concerns about your choice in a mate, the odds are pretty good that this person is not the right one for you.

You might be thinking to yourself, This is my decision and no one can make it for me. We couldn't agree with you more, but don't you think it might be in your best interest to take into consideration what your loved ones have to say about your decision to be with this guy?

Every single one of these women's friends was right, and yours probably are, too. They aren't jealous or vengeful. They aren't trying to make your life miserable; you are doing a fine job of that yourself! *You* are the one with the blinders on. So if more than one of your friends or family members has shared their concerns with you, honestly reflect on what they have to say. How do their concerns match up to your gut feelings? Listen closely. Your happiness depends on it.

The Solution Is Within You

No matter what the reason, it's never easy to call off a wedding. But don't make the same mistake so many women in this book did. Carefully consider your concerns and ask yourself the tough questions. Unfortunately, there is no one-size-fits-all strategy that will give you the courage to call off your wedding. Each woman's situation is unique. What we *can* tell you is that you *already have the courage within you.* It's there. Every woman within these pages had the courage to dodge that bullet, but not all of them could find it at the time.

Let's review those steps you need to take:

Step 1: Give yourself some time to just think about calling it off.

Step 2: Say the words out loud: "I want to call it off."

Step 3: Take action: The secret is to do *something*!

It's not too late! You can do this! Learn from the mistakes of others. Listen to their advice. Stop making excuses, and let go of your fears. Call upon the courageous part within you and trust that it will guide you to do what's right. It's time to put your happiness back in your *own* hands.

PART 5

✦

How
to Find
the *Right* Guy

✦ 9 ✦

Marriage Material
Words of Wisdom on Choosing a Spouse

A woman has got to love a bad man once or
twice in her life, to be thankful for a good one.
—Marjorie Kinnan Rawlings

If You Need More Help Deciding

We've talked about the mistakes women make that put them
at risk of marrying the wrong guys. We've told you about red
flags and gut feelings. We've clarified the difference between
cold feet and jitters. We've shared with you stories of women
who ended their relationships or canceled their weddings,
and we've shared stories of the women who did not. There is
a lot for you to think about. But we've got one final trick up
our sleeves. We are now going to share the collective wisdom
of dozens and dozens of *happily married women*. They share
their stories to demonstrate that you, too, can someday marry
the right guy.

Some of the women we interviewed have been married
just five years and some for almost fifty years. We eliminated

...an who said she had the "perfect marriage," because ...o such thing and we doubted the wisdom of anyone who made this claim. Instead, we talked to women who identified themselves as "happily married." Sure, they go through the same ups and downs, dry spells, and aggravation that we all do. But overall, they say they are very happy, con-

✦ ✦ ✦ ✦

How to Marry a Stable Man

- Seek out a reliable man.
- Fall in love with a good listener.
- Understand the importance of loving a man you can always count on.

That way, when someone asks you what you love about him, you'll say:

My husband is quiet and is a good listener. He is helpful and tries hard to please. He is fair with the children, both biological and step. He is a constant. Knowing that I have an attentive ear helps me to deal with problems that arise both at home and away from home. Being able to rely on my husband to help around the house—with the children and in other areas of our lives—enables me to get involved in things outside the home and have a well-rounded lifestyle. I can count on my husband in any situation, which is comforting and relaxing. All of these things help me be a good me. If I weren't a good me, I wouldn't make a good wife or mother.

✦

tent, and grateful for their husbands. It was fun to have a flood of *positive* surveys fill up our mailboxes. One woman said that she had initially hesitated to complete the survey because she had been irritated with her husband for a few days. She called back when she was done and said it was just what she needed to do because it reminded her of all of his wonderful characteristics!

Look in the Mirror

Sometimes you need to look at your relationship differently to see it as it really is. You need to hold it up to a mirror to see its flaws or to determine what is missing. These positive testimonies are that mirror.

There is no checklist that exists that will detail what *you* need for a happy marriage. Everyone has a different idea about what they want in a spouse. As one woman told us, "He is not a perfect man, but he is the perfect man for me."

We each have different wants, needs, concerns, and desires. By reading the words of wisdom from a broad cross section of happily married women, you may be able to uncover what is wrong or missing in your current relationship. You might also become more aware of what a great guy you do have. But more important, you will learn how to articulate your vision for what you want and need in a future partner or husband.

We asked happily married women to share what they've learned about creating a fulfilling marriage. They share what they value most about their spouses and what they've learned,

offer words of wisdom for young women contem-
harriage.

✦   ✦   ✦   ✦

How to Marry a Man You Can Depend On

- Date a guy who keeps his promises.
- Fall in love with a man who pays his bills on time.
- Seek a boyfriend who has a lot of friends—friends that you like.
- Find a man who makes you laugh.

That way, when someone asks you what you love about him, you'll say:

My husband is committed—our family and our relationship come first. He will speak up even to family when their actions or words interfere with how we believe. He is thoughtful. He may not be a big romantic, but he knows when to surprise me with a clean bathroom or dinner for two—or when to give me space. He is also funny—oh so funny, with everyone in all situations. He may go over the line sometimes, but his humor solves more problems than it causes.

✦

The Right Guy: What's He Like?

There are certain qualities that we all know are important in a spouse. Some of the bedrock characteristics include com-passion, honesty, and respect. These are a given. But there are a lot of other qualities and traits that are necessary for a good, transformative marriage. Unfortunately, we don't always know what qualities we really want and need until we're trapped in bad marriages or relationships. So let's hear it from happily married women. What are their spouses' best characteristics and how do they benefit their marriages?

My husband is intelligent, ambitious, kind, humorous, physically active, supportive, spiritual, and very forgiving. I share a love of nature and outdoor activities with him, and I appreciate his knowledge about science and business. Humor has been our antidote for pain and anger.

My husband is gentle and patient. He is a good man with a lot of integrity, and he works hard at being a good husband. He is not a perfect man, but he is the perfect man for me. He listens to me, tries to understand my moods, and sometimes just asks what he can do to help me. Other than my parents, I have never had someone love me as deeply as I know he does. Sure, we argue, and we get on one another's nerves, but we always know it is temporary. Our relationship is built on the trust that we are both committed to one another. We have been married only five years, but I can honestly say that we have never had an argument so intense that I worried we wouldn't make it. Divorce or leaving one another is just not an option for us. We work at things until we resolve them. While that isn't always easy, our marriage is important enough for both of us to do so.

He is very kind and forgiving, and he thoroughly loves being a husband and father and grandpa.

He does not respond to events with anger, and he never uses criticism or shame as a method of fighting. He can hold his own and argue his position with kindness and is often insightful and correct in his perspective. He is confident of his own views yet has the grace and stability to allow divergence and alternative points of view. He takes charge when he needs to and has the grace to use problem-solving skills when I am out of sorts. He matches my moods and laughs often and well at the world's choices. He is also gorgeous at seventy-plus and continues to explore new ideas with amazing enthusiasm.

He is level-headed and logical whereas I am emotional. It balances out when we are making major decisions together. I appreciate that he is like that, because it brings me back down to earth and defines things more clearly when I am stuck on the emotional side of a problem or decision.

My husband is very comfortable with who he is, and he doesn't feel pressure to meet others' expectations. As someone who is always trying to please everyone, I find that refreshing! One of the first things that attracted me to him was his broad range of friends. He invited me to a backyard barbecue, and the group consisted of an incredibly diverse mix of people (especially for Boston) from different races, backgrounds, creeds, careers, ages, nationalities, and abilities/disabilities. I had never been to a house gathering that was so interesting—and comfortable. "Who is this guy," I wondered, "who cultivates a wonderful group of friends like this?" He really sees the best in all people first and considers everyone his friend—unless or until they prove otherwise. Just as he is who he is, he sees others for who they are—not what they do, who they know, etc. He's kind, particularly to those in need. He's down-to-earth and practical—and yet has a spiritual side. We share a sense of adventure, and of actively "building" a life, not just waiting for it to happen. He's goofy and funny in a way that totally cracks me up.

He is the kindest person I have ever known. I can count on him to be truthful with me, and he listens. When we have hit some difficulty, those qualities shine through, so we can deal with the problem and not have to deal with his reaction to the problem before we can tackle the issue. He is really smart and sexy, too. So it is hard to stay mad at him for very long.

He is the voice of reason. He rarely gets rattled about anything. While I am freaking out or overreacting, he always puts things into perspective.

His priorities are in order—faith, family, and friends. He has a great sense of humor. He is intelligent, calm, and a good listener (which goes very well with a talker like me!).

He is intelligent and has multiple interests. He is a fabulous listener and communicator. We have many of the same interests, and he is always willing to try new adventures. We enjoy spending time together, whether we are just "being" or actually participating in an activity. We do not argue very much at all, because he is always willing to talk about my concerns and feelings, and we often agree to disagree.

✦   ✦   ✦   ✦

Anne's Story: My Dad's Character

My mom knew a good thing when she saw it. My dad is a real sweetheart. He is an honest, sensitive, and caring man. It's not hard to see what kind of person he is—his actions always show it. Little things mean a lot.

As a child I can clearly remember my dad driving all the way back to the grocery store after the clerk had given him too much change. It was no more than two dollars, but he knew the clerk had made a mistake and would be charged for it. It was not his money, so he drove all the way back to the store and returned it. That really made an impression on me. It was a small deed but a large indicator of my father's character.

Another way my father shows his character is in the way he honors his family obligations. My mother passed away a few years ago, but my dad still looks after my aunts—my mother's sisters. One of her sisters is disabled. My dad helps supervise her care. He makes sure she keeps busy and all is well in her apartment. He has her over for dinner. He helps pay her bills and does her taxes.

Recently this same aunt decided to attend her high school reunion. My dad was concerned about her, so he said he would be her date. He gave up his Saturday night and dressed up in his spiffy blue blazer and a tie and escorted her to the reunion. He was afraid she would be uncomfortable and would want him to be close by. He walked her in, made sure everything was okay, and then sat out in his car reading a book. She ended up having a great time. He was on standby for her—just in case she needed him. That's the kind of man you want to marry. You want to marry the guy who will take your disabled sister to her high school reunion even after you are gone.

✦

Does a Twenty-Year-Old Woman Want the Same Things as a Seventy-Year-Old Woman?

We asked women to think back to when they were in their early twenties. We were curious about what they looked for in dates or boyfriends. What did their twenty-year-old selves think was important? Were the qualities they desired back then still important to them now?

When I was younger and shallower, physical appearance was a big issue. If I were to find myself looking today—which I have no intention of doing—I would be more likely to look for someone who would be a good provider, someone mature, someone with strong moral values, a witty sense of humor, and intelligence.

This question made me realize how very much I have changed in twenty years! When I was twenty, I wanted a good-looking, well-built guy who liked to go out and have fun and who had money to spend on me. Now, the qualities that I think are important in a good spouse are love, commitment, responsibility, friendship, and shared dreams and values.

I wanted smart, funny, sensitive, and kind. I wanted to be very important to that person. Those qualities were important to me then and are important to me now.

Honesty was a really important characteristic, and so was over-all goodness. I tended to date gregarious, life-of-the-party type guys who were arrogant. I married the complete opposite, and I feel extremely grateful.

Then, I think having fun and finding someone "sexy" was major. I do think my husband of twenty-eight years is sexy, but now a level head and "wisdom" are more important to me.

I think when I was younger, I had a list in my head of characteristics: ambitious, likes to do the things I do, and makes me laugh. I didn't think as much about the qualities of the man as a person, but more about what he did, and how that related to me. Now, I think more about who he is, alone with me, and in the world. Qualities such as kindness and curiosity (about other people and the world) are important. Other important considerations include being loving to his family, conscientiousness, spirituality, and humor. Yes, humor is still a key ingredient!

The qualities I looked for then are the same qualities that are important now. Great sense of humor, kind, honest/ethical, God at the center of his heart, fun, someone who enjoys sports and staying active (and good-looking). Most important, someone who likes to laugh! Someone who has many friends.

I think I often fell into relationships where I had to "fix" someone. After a few bad relationships I timed myself out and stopped worrying about being with someone. In the end what I needed was a man who was at least as strong as I am and who wasn't needy or undependable. Now the most important qualities are strength, humor, and love. I married my husband without any expectations that he would change.

Looks were probably more important to me when I was younger than when I got older, though it wasn't critical even then. Kindness and compassion were always important to me. I was taught early on to look hard at the parents of anyone I dated—it would tell me a lot about that person. I noticed immediately how close his family was and what a good marriage his parents seemed to have, even though they certainly had their noisy Italian arguments. They reminded me of my parents.

When I was twenty, I was dating a very attractive but boring man. I remember my friends asking me what I liked most about him and my only response was always, "He's just so cute." I had no concept of what I wanted or needed in a relationship and, needless to say, we broke up. I constantly picked fights with this guy, just to provoke emotion from him. I needed more than just good looks, and even though I knew it, I refused to let go of him because he was cute! *Being cute is still an important quality, but I've learned that it really means nothing. Looks fade, but a person who gets who I am and can hold up his end of a conversation and make me laugh—that is what really matters to me now.*

No matter what your age, it's important to consider the traits you want and need in your future spouse or boyfriend.

at is your vision for your married life? What do you need for a fulfilling relationship? Good looks and sexiness are not enough. One woman sums it up best:

I needed competence and still do. I needed kindness and still do. I needed caretaking and still do. The twenty and the seventy are not that far apart.

✦   ✦   ✦   ✦

Anne's Story: Why You Must Marry a Man You Can Always Count On

My sweet husband—the right guy—and I went through *a lot* the first five years of our marriage. We experienced good times and bad, sickness and health, and both ends of the "for richer and poorer" spectrum! The challenges we faced showed me what a truly amazing man he is and how lucky I am to be married to him. When I sum up what I love most about Doug, it's hard to choose. He loves me, he respects me, and he makes me laugh every day. But there is something else that I've discovered that is necessary for a solid marriage. You need to be able to count on your husband to do the right thing. Whether it is honoring family obligations, working overtime, or helping out a neighbor—he needs to be rock solid. It's OK if he complains a little bit—just as long as you know that in the end he will do what is right.

His integrity helps me to be a better person. When I am thinking, "Well, maybe I will just skip that funeral and send a card," he'll gently remind me how much it means to be there.

Or I'll say, "I don't really want to do such and such," and he will point out why I should. Usually I can't resist because I know that he practices what he preaches. This is so important— especially as you get older and face more life challenges. Caring for an aging or sick parent, treating a life-threatening illness, or dealing with teenagers can be hard enough without the love and support of your partner. Knowing you can always depend on your spouse brings a sense of peace to your life.

I decided to talk to a few women who understand the importance of reliability and integrity. Here is what Jennifer's mother-in-law said about her beloved now-deceased husband:

He was an honest, polite, kind man with a terrific sense of humor, but above all else he never wavered in his love for me and his family. He always provided for us. He was by no means a saint, just a good man. I think his commitment to the success and safety of me and our kids gave our marriage a sense of peace, trust, and security.

They were high school sweethearts and were married for more than forty years. His commitment to his family created a marriage that *still* serves as a model for all of their children. Another friend of mine whose husband is facing the challenges of a degenerative neuromuscular disease weighed in:

His best characteristics are his faithfulness and humbleness. He is faithful to his family and always makes sure that we are second in his life—right after God. He has such a humble nature. He never complains about his health or the unfairness of the cards he has been dealt. He has such a giving nature, but in a most quiet manner. He always does kind deeds without ever looking for acknowledgment.

In spite of his declining mobility, he still gets up every day and goes to work. His commitment makes this incredible challenge a bit easier to bear.

My cousin is an oncology nurse. She provides bedside care to cancer patients in the final days of their lives. I asked her to share her insights after witnessing some of the most difficult days in a married couple's life—when they have to say good-bye.

What strikes me the most is that for some couples it is simply about being there for one another. It's not about the big gestures, the over-the-top bouquets of flowers or things like that. It is about spending every last bit of time they have—together. I have watched husbands offer such loving, tender care. It is so beautiful. They gently wipe the brows of their wives, straighten the bedcovers, or offer small sips of water. There is no other place that they would rather be. I have come to believe that this sense of peace and serenity in the final days is an extension of what their marriage was like. They both know that they can rely on one another. They trust one another—and they both take great comfort knowing that they are preparing each other for the next step of their journey.

What a beautiful testimony to the strength and power of a loving marriage. What is most telling about her observation is that it articulates the value of sharing your life with someone who loves and cherishes you. A spouse you can count on will give you the strength you need to get through anything . . . even when that means saying good-bye.

✦

How Have Happy Marriages Influenced You?

Living in the reflected glow of a happy marriage can have a positive influence on your own relationship. It's important to realize, however, that your parents' happy marriage does not inoculate you from the possibility of divorce. Likewise, children of divorce are not always doomed to unhappy marriages of their own. What's *most* important is that you're *aware* of what a happy marriage looks and feels like. Let's take a look at how the happy marriages in these women's lives influenced their own.

My parents are happily married and have been for more than forty years. That is not to say they have not had their share of ups and downs, but they have stuck by each other even when one has let the other down. They have forgiven each other, laughed at their differences, and griped about them, too, but they still manage to hold each other's hand when walking together. This has made a huge impact in my life and the marriage I now have.

Almost everyone I knew growing up had a happy marriage, or at least from what I observed. I grew up surrounded by good, solid families that really showed me how important a strong foundation is. I valued how most of my friends grew up, and I wanted the same for our kids.

Many of our friends have happy marriages. It seems the key is respect for the other person, knowing that their weaknesses are probably your strengths and not something you have to change. We each have the missing pieces that the other one does not have.

The happy marriages I see are between people who have stable individual personalities. They share child rearing, chores, and other practical things, and have similar worldviews. They also seem to share a willingness to change together.

My parents and grandparents enjoyed one another's company and made each other a priority. It has helped me look forward to my life with my husband, seeing couples who are successfully growing old together. It gives me hope. I have a forty-eight-year-old friend who is now caring for her formerly athletic and active husband who is in a skilled nursing facility due to suffering a traumatic brain injury in a motor vehicle crash. It is hard, but the love is still observable between them. It has shown me that even in the worst of times, a strong and loving marriage makes anything tolerable.

I think my model for a happy marriage was my grandparents. They were married for seventy-five years! They were both strong and independent people who really cared for each other. They were funny together, and never really "lovey" or affectionate in front of us kids, but you could tell these two people would do anything for each other. They also totally put up with each other's quirks. I know they didn't have an easy life together, especially early on; there were several miscarriages and many disagreements. However, they were committed to many of the same things—a strong and healthy family above all. They also had their own interests. They died within twelve hours of each other, the day before Valentine's Day. The impact on me was that I understood and believed that a happy marriage could exist, but it wouldn't be idyllic! It also made me feel safe and comfortable and loved—and I came to recognize that feeling when I met "the one."

We have friends who got married at eighteen due to a pregnancy and have been truly happy for thirty-five years. With everything pushing against them, they pulled together. They still play like a couple of kids. They respect and adore one another. There is nothing worse than a bad marriage, but a good one is one of life's great blessings. I have been married now for twenty-four years and wake up each day feeling loved.

The neighbors next door exemplify the love, courage, and faith it takes to have a truly great marriage. We have shared good times and bad times. They have taught me that in spite of great hardship, love and faith are always with us; they laugh even when they cry. I have come to realize that even when you think it is as bad as it could be, you can still love one another.

I was very blessed to witness my parents' marriage. They certainly lived through some really difficult times, and I witnessed some of those. Yet they modeled for my siblings and me how to work things out, rely on their faith, and so on. My dad always called my mom his "bride." It was clear that they loved each other. They were also quite affectionate—too much in my adolescent eyes sometimes.

...arents' marriage of fifty years has been a true inspiration to me. I have seen their love for one another blossom over the years, and it just keeps getting stronger. They have had a happy, faith-filled, loving relationship, and even though they have been through much sadness (their fourth daughter had Down syndrome and was a precious angel lost at the tender age of eleven; they also endured the deaths of their parents and a sibling), they have never lost sight of the love they have for one another. My parents have always backed one another up when it came to raising their daughters, even if they didn't always agree with each

✦   ✦   ✦   ✦

How to Marry a Great Dad

- Observe how your boyfriend interacts with your nieces and nephews—and then like what you see.
- Date a man who values his family.
- Choose a man who is active and likes to try new things.
- Seek a man who is slow to anger.

That way, when someone asks you what you love about him, you'll say:

He is a man of the highest integrity; he is as solid as a rock when it comes to life's issues. He has a good sense of humor and enjoys the simple things in life, like being with the kids or working outside. I never have to worry about him or how he will weigh in on an issue. I can count on him, and he always sees things with great clarity. This helps us to work through issues without a lot of drama.

✦

other. They always kept a unified front, and my husband and I try to incorporate that gift into our marriage today.

My parents just celebrated their fortieth anniversary. They truly love and support each other. I don't know what the next forty years will hold, but it's my intention to do everything I can to get to my fortieth anniversary with my husband.

Words of Wisdom on Choosing a Spouse

We've heard the words of wisdom from women who were married to the wrong guy. Now let's hear from some happily married women. What wise words do they offer on choosing the right guy? What's important? What should you think about?

Don't marry someone thinking you will change him. God created them as they are and you won't be able to undo him.

Romance, good looks, and sex will diminish over time. Make sure your relationship includes important factors such as friendship, a shared interest in things, companionship, and genuine love for one another.

Before you slip the ring on your finger or say "I do," make sure to ask yourself these questions. Does he treat his mom with respect? Does he treat his dog with respect? Does he actually listen to other people or does he just act like he does? Is he ethical in business? Is he spiritual? Can he balance his checkbook? Do you feel good about yourself when you are with him? Does he know how to make a bed? Does he really know who you are? If you answer no to any of these questions, run the other way!

Make sure you feel like you are yourself around him. Don't morph into something you are not, because you will only regret it in the future. Try to find a balance between what he can offer you and how you can complement him. You can't put yourself first all the time, but you can't always put his needs first either. There needs to be a compromise at all times, and keeping track of who "won" last time won't get you anywhere. Make sure you love his not-so-great qualities, too, because they don't go away!

Share common interests and values—friendship. And be able to laugh at yourself and each other. Be able to forgive yourself and your spouse.

Be open—your Prince Charming may not appear the way you have pictured him! Know yourself first, and then be curious about others. Don't expect that a spouse will fill all the gaps in your life, or be your perfect companion in every way—and don't let them make that mistake either. Pick someone who truly "gets" you, understands your strengths and weaknesses, and respects and admires you, and vice versa! Be up-front in discussing issues such as money, children, and in-laws, so you are both clear on what you'll tolerate and what you can't. Not everyone defines marriage the same way. Make sure you're on the same ground before making the commitment. Don't base your decision on looks, money, status, or anything else that can change—because they will; you need to make sure that if all those were gone, you would still want to be with him.

I tell my children to start with happy. Choose someone who is naturally good-natured. You can't make someone happy, so it's better to start with that. Be happy yourself. Choose generous. If a person can't part with money, they won't be generous in other areas either. Money is the easiest thing to give away so pay attention. Stingy shows up everywhere, in sharing yourself, in helping with the chores, in time with you and the children.

Make sure you are crazy about him and he is crazy about you. Make sure that you have the same goals. Talk about your goals, wants, and dreams. Think about having children with this person and getting old with this person. Loving them forever. If that does not sound like something that makes you happy, then you are not ready for marriage.

Make sure he is kind, treats you with respect, and is faithful and truthful to you. And make sure his love for you is as deeply rooted as your love is for him.

Choose someone who makes you laugh. Share some common interests. Know that what attracts you to that person will probably at some point irritate you. This is not a bad thing, though it is the very thing that creates a spiritual partner—someone who challenges you to grow and know yourself better.

The person you marry should be a match for you in the following ways: love, sex, money, and children. And he must match in all four. You can be sexually compatible with a person, but if he's broke and needs you to take care of him, say good-bye. It is so important that you hash all of these issues out before *the wedding.*

Make sure you both agree on how to spend and save money. Make sure he knows that you want to be a stay-at-home mom after the second kid. Make sure he loves you for who you are and exactly that. Make sure he knows what you like in and out of the bedroom and supports your ambitions. And you should be able to say the very same for yourself concerning him.

Choose a man you respect, deeply love, and a man who wants to take care of you and your family. Don't marry someone who has an annoying habit you can't stand now, because it will only drive you crazy later. Marry the love of your life, a man you cannot live without, a man you would never want to let down, a man you want to love and cherish. Marry a man who already is a good friend to his friends and respects his mother. These are the characteristics of a good man who is marriage material.

✦　✦　✦　✦

Jen's Story: My Happy Marriage

Once I hit my late teens, I was pretty confident in what I wanted in a boyfriend. He would have to respect me, make me laugh, and above all, accept all of me, inside and out. There was also a big part of me that was looking for someone to rescue me and get me the hell out of my house. By the time I went off to college, it was pretty obvious that my parents were not happy and the thought of returning to that environment was depressing. I am not particularly proud of that part of me, but it was reality.

I met my husband in high school and was immediately attracted to him, "metal mouth" and all. He was and continues to be a charmer! My dad used to call him "Eddie Haskell" (the insincere brownnoser from *Leave It to Beaver*). I never liked it when he called him that because it made him seem false; in reality, he just did nice things for people. Back then I think my dad was skeptical of such behavior. When we first started dating, I was introduced to his enormous family. Many of his brothers and sisters had already gotten married and started having children. I had never seen a teenage boy hold a baby and actually enjoy it! I remember thinking what a great dad he would grow up to be, and I was right. He held the door open for me, he liked my friends, he didn't judge my family, he never embarrassed me, he respected me, and he was a good person. It did not hurt that he was tall, dark, and handsome! Those qualities were and continue to be attractive. Another important quality is his ability to forgive me, as well as take responsibility for his own mistakes.

We dated for seven years before we got married. We were young and naive but we never doubted the decision we were making. Although my parents had a difficult relationship, his parents had a wonderful marriage. He brought that experience of living in a loving marriage to our relationship.

When we first got married, we were broke and lived in a teeny-tiny apartment. Despite the small size of our home, for the first time in my life, I felt like I had some breathing room. I often felt like I had to walk on pins and needles in my parents' home, never knowing when things were going to "blow." When the volcano would erupt it would suck the life out of me. I had no idea how hard it was to breathe in that environment. I was always holding my breath, waiting for the eruption once again. The day I moved into that apartment, I immediately became more relaxed, no longer anticipating the worst.

Besides giving me space to breathe, my husband has also given me unconditional love, respect, laughter, and the ultimate gift, forgiveness. Fifteen years later, we have survived the loss of his father, my parents' divorce, the purchase of our first house, health issues, job issues, the birth of our beautiful children, and financial stress. Yet through all of the joy and sadness, I have never once questioned his love for me and his faith in our relationship. And we celebrate each passing year as if it is the first. (The right guy will *never* forget your anniversary!)

The one challenge we had then and continue to work on today is how we deal with conflict. He rarely watched his parents argue, and I learned that the safest response to conflict was to run and hide. Needless to say, when a conflict erupts in our relationship today, I typically want to escape. You can imagine how well that goes over in our house! What he has shown me, however, is that no matter what, we will deal with our difficulties head-on. He gives me time to retreat for a little while but then he gently wrangles me back in and we work it through, even if we agree to disagree. I never fear that he'll abandon me for having a different thought, opinion, or approach than he does. This is a complete 360-degree turn from what I observed in my parents' house. Conflict would flare up, tempers would soar, and resentments would stay bottled up until the cork eventually flew off that day in my parents' living room. I made a commitment to myself and to my husband to approach conflict differently, no matter how hard it might be. It is a commitment that we revisit often, sometimes even when we do it wrong.

I share my story with you so that you might start to t
into the part of you that wants a healthy marriage and to
just end up another divorce statistic. My life could have turned
out very differently if my husband had not shown up or if I had
not paid attention to him when he did enter into my life. There
were plenty of wrong guys out there, and they were seductive.
In my gut, I knew better than to throw a good thing away.
And although I would have gladly let him rescue me from my
dreaded castle, he knew what I needed and has been right by
my side while I learn how to "rescue" myself. For that I am
grateful.

✦

✦　✦　✦　✦

How to Marry an Honest Man

- Fall in love with a man of integrity.
- Look for a boyfriend who always tells the truth.
- Understand the importance of a sense of humor.

That way, when someone asks you what you love about him,
you'll say:

*My husband is honest. I can always trust his words; I never have to
doubt or wonder. This provides security, which is a must in a strong
relationship. He is also humorous. His ability to bring lighthearted
fun and laughter to a situation makes life more bearable. And he is
sensitive. Knowing he cares and is emotionally invested in our life
together allows for intimacy.*

✦

Words of Wisdom and Advice from the Clergy

Many marriages are officiated by a priest or pastor. Not only do they preside over the wedding ceremony itself, but they are often involved with some sort of marriage preparation. The Roman Catholic faith requires all engaged couples to participate in a course of marriage preparation. Other faiths offer similar classes or require that a couple meet privately with their pastor or officiant several times prior to the wedding. We discussed misguided marriages with a Catholic priest and a Presbyterian pastor, and we found that their insights and observations were surprisingly similar. Notice that both of them feel very strongly about the benefits of marriage preparation. They believe that couples who approach marriage with a *shared* commitment to success have a better chance of a happy, fulfilling relationship. Here are a few excerpts from those interviews.

Marriage Insights from Father Jim

✦

*C*atholics preparing for marriage usually complete a FOCCUS (Facilitating Open Couple Communication, Understanding, and Study) questionnaire. People always refer to the FOCCUS as a test. It is actually not a test—it is a tool for generating discussion. It is a good tool and a useful instrument. However, it can only identify potential conflicts; it doesn't solve them. One of the most important questions on the FOCCUS instrument is "I value keeping peace at any price." No one should agree with this. Because if you do, you are agreeing to live with something you can't bear, just to avoid a fight. Unfortunately, our culture often encourages us to say *anything* to get past an unpleasant situation in which you find yourself. The best-case scenario with marriage preparation is that a couple discovers issues they have not resolved—and then deals with them.

My dominant impression of engaged couples is that *people have no idea what they are getting into*! Sharing lives, sharing intimacy—it is harder work than a person could imagine. American society does not prepare us to get married as well as it should. Not many people grow up in households with both a father and a mother these days—this does not allow for role modeling. People must understand that being raised in a solid, loving family shows a person how marriage is done. But if you do not have this role model, it doesn't mean you are doomed to failure; you must simply be aware of this missing insight.

I believe that the idea that marriage is about sharing and sacrifice has fallen out of favor. It is important to have a shared commitment to the institution of marriage. Love is a decision. You must begin every day by deciding again, "I am going to love you."

Do not get married if you have doubts. If you are uncertain, you need to work it out. Don't get married just because you have the reception hall rented. This is not a good enough reason to spend your life in misery. You may be able to resolve the doubts you are having; however, do it *before* the wedding because it may not be possible *after.* I tell couples that they must be mature enough to make the decision to marry. They must have the maturity and commitment to back up their decision. It's also important to be truly good friends—not just hormones that like each other. Are you comfortable just "hanging out" with each other? The bottom line is that your marriage has potential to make you both miserable, so it's not something to jump into if you have any doubts.

Marriage Insights from Pastor Joe

✦

I am always glad when couples are interested in really working through things and talking about their relationships. Why? Because 75 percent of engaged couples are not interested in premarital counseling. They are more concerned with wedding plans, caterers, colors, and flowers. They are not engaged in the counseling, and their hearts are not in it. In order for counseling to be effective, they have to be receptive, or it simply does not work. They are usually just going through the motions; they want to get it checked off the list. Something that strikes me, as a man of the cloth so to speak, is that people usually try to reserve the reception site first, and then they reserve the church. It's kind of symbolic of their priorities.

I have the right to refuse to marry people, and I have done that twice in thirty-five years. The first time, the groom showed up drunk. I did not marry them and had the full support of every single guest. The couple married later, but the marriage did not last long. The other time it was due to abuse. I knew that the bride lived in an abusive home and was trying to escape this—but she was about to marry an abusive person. I witnessed verbal abuse and saw signs of physical abuse on her. They got married anyway; unfortunately, I do not know what happened to her.

Some of the happiest people I know, people with wonderful marriages, don't have a lot of material wealth. They don't need it. Their solid, healthy marriage brings them all the joy and happiness they need. There are other people I know who have lots of material things, but no joy. It is an interesting lesson.

When we want to learn how to do something new, we seek out training and guidance. For example, if someone wants to become a real estate agent, they attend classes and take a test in order to obtain a license. It's a requirement for the job. They may also seek out a mentor in the field—someone who can show them how to navigate all the potential problems and issues that can arise when selling property. The more prepared they are, the better their chances of a successful real estate career. Men and women should approach marriage preparation with the same desire to succeed. Brides- and grooms-to-be should be willing do the necessary work to prepare for a successful marriage.

I believe that when people are more intentional and see a counselor before marriage, they have a better chance of finding that biblical sense of "shalom"—peace—in their marriage. With preparation, they will find a true sense of contentment, happiness, and serenity when the two become one.

Words of Wisdom on Marriage

What wise words would our happily married women offer a young woman about marriage; once she has decided to marry the *right* guy?

Marriage is wonderful, difficult, all-consuming, and can be completely satisfying. It is a work in progress every day! If you put as much work into the actual marriage as you do in the planning of the wedding, you will be OK.

Marriage is perhaps the most important decision in life. Know yourself well and know realistically what you need out of a relationship. Can this person meet your needs?

As wonderful as you may envision marriage to be, it is that much better. And as hard as you think marriage is going to be, it is that much harder. You don't make your marriage vows only on your wedding day; you spend each day of your marriage living out the "for better or for worse, for richer or for poorer, and in sickness and in health."

Bring your faith into your marriage, really listen to the vows you are taking at your wedding, and know that each day of marriage is a recommitment to those vows. Know that all the conflicts and hard times in your marriage are what make you fall deeper in love if you stick it out. The good times are precious, but the hard times are what mold two hearts into one.

Plan on marriage being a lifetime commitment. Make sure, as much as you can, that this is someone you want to live with for a long time, and be willing to grow old with him. Plan to not always get your way—figure that if you each give in on things that are really important to the other (presuming you can, in integrity), you can compromise on most issues that come up. Be willing to talk about things. Want to make the other person happy, but be sure you know how to be happy yourself. And know that there will be days/times when you won't be crazy about him; but know that that, too, is part of the ebb and flow of relationships.

Take time to enjoy yourselves as a couple, no matter how hard your jobs are or how many children you have.

Remind yourself it is forever. And anything that lasts forever must be well cared for. Listen to the logical side of your heart. When you sense huge red flags, know that they will not go away.

Remind yourself every day that you are a 50 percent shareholder in the company, which means that if you truly put your heart and soul into the relationship, there is a huge possibility that it will be successful.

Enter into marriage as a commitment rather than a trial, and know that marriage reflects the rest of life: It includes pain, struggle, and change. If there is no openness to change there can be no growth. Love changes faces—from early passion to a deep and abiding respect. You may not always feel like you are in love.

Marriage is at its core a partnership. It helps if you share some of the same values and goals. But it's also important for each partner to bring something special to the relationship—complementary skills, experiences, knowledge. If something drives you crazy about the person (he's a slob, she talks too much, whatever), it's only going to get more pronounced as you're together. Sometimes people can make small changes, but chances are, you're going to have to live with it! So decide before you make the commitment if this is something you can live with!

In the '70s when I was in high school, a teacher once gave me some advice, long before the phrase "What would Jesus do?" became popular. I was having a problem with a friend and he said, "Look at all the ways you can solve this. Then choose the most loving thing to do." Those words really stayed with me, and I find that they work in our relationship as well. We don't keep score; we just respond with love and kindness. Laughter is essential. Whatever is horrible today won't be as big or scary tomorrow.

A healthy marriage takes work. Both people have to be willing to work at it, make changes, forgive, grow together, and so forth. Faith is a critical piece and a wonderful gift to a marriage. Look to healthy models of marriage as guides for how to overcome the tough times.

Be very sure that you want a marriage, not just a wedding. The wedding is one day; the marriage is your whole life. If you just want a wedding, throw yourself a party and wear a white dress.

Marriage is an exciting, wonderfully frustrating learning experience. Be prepared to learn about yourself and the man you married and respond with laughter, loads of patience, some tears and frustration, but plenty of love. You will learn about the many depths of love, and it will change your life forever. Tend to your heart and his, be patient, and give all that you can and more, and you will reap unbelievable love.

✦ 10 ✦

Avoiding the Biggest Mistake
of Your Life
A Recap of Questions and Action Steps

So How Do You Marry the *Right* Guy?

We believe wholeheartedly in the institution of marriage, whether that is the sacrament that is shared in the front of your church, the vows you make in front of your community of friends and loved ones, or the promises you make to each other in front of the Elvis impersonator who works nights at the Little Chapel on the Vegas strip. We believe that every woman deserves to be in a happy, healthy relationship. We want you to believe that for yourself.

Dozens of women have revisited their own painful pasts (and joyful presents), in order to help you make the right decisions about your own relationship. We sincerely hope that you have taken their advice to heart and will apply it to your own life. Learn from their mistakes. Learn from your own mistakes. Take this knowledge and put it to good use. Don't stay stuck in an unhealthy or unhappy relationship. Put the wheels in motion *now* and begin that journey toward having the relationship that you have always wanted but never believed possible. *Marrying the right guy begins with you.*

Have you gained an understanding of what you want and need in a partner? Have you defined a clearer vision of the life you want—and the kind of husband or partner you need to achieve this vision? Let's clarify something: Women don't *need* a man in order to be happy. But if marriage is part of your life plan, make sure you are not jumping into marriage for the wrong reasons, with the wrong man.

We want you to marry the right *guy,* the man who will add to your life, not subtract from it. Take the time right now to revisit the questions we asked throughout this book. Go through each of the five parts one more time. Your answers will help you avoid making the biggest mistake of your life.

Part 1: How Not to Date the Wrong Guy

What can you do to make sure you are not dating the wrong guy?

1. Think about the reasons that you said yes to a second date with a guy who did not make a great impression on you. Did you say yes to a third or fourth date? Why or why not?

2. Think about red flags you have observed in former or current boyfriends. What were they?

3. Think about your deal breakers. Have you ever continued to date a guy even though you knew there was a serious problem, such as emotional abuse or active addiction?

What can you do to make sure you date the right guy?

1. Think about some previous relationships that didn't work out. Did you stay for any of the following reasons?

- Did you feel lonely and insecure?
- Did you think the relationship could solve your problems?
- Did you feel external pressures to stay in the relationship?
- Did you think he would fix you / you would fix him?
- Did you ignore red flags and gut feelings?

2. Were there other reasons? What were they?

3. Hold on to what is important to you. Don't change your personality. Don't lower your standards. Be conscious of what you want and what your values are.

4. It is important to know what a healthy relationship looks like. After fifteen years of working with couples, and countless hours of research, we have observed the following characteristics in healthy relationships. How many of these qualities can you find in your current relationship?

- You bring out the best in each other, not the worst.
- You trust each other; each can count on the other to do the right thing.
- You both appreciate each other's authenticity and allow each other to be autonomous.
- You appreciate all the parts that make your partner whole without needing him to change, or vice versa.
- You do thoughtful things for each other without asking for anything in return (or keeping score!).

- You have fun together.
- You genuinely miss each other when you are apart.
- You share common core beliefs and values.
- Sexual intimacy may not always be a roaring fire, but when it dies down, the glowing embers are easily stoked!

✦   ✦   ✦   ✦

How to Marry a Man Who Cherishes You

- Look for a man who accepts you as you are.
- Fall in love with a man who thinks you are beautiful on the inside and outside.
- Seek a boyfriend who is loving and forgiving.
- Understand the importance of a good sense of humor.

That way, when someone asks you what you love about him, you'll say:

My husband has a great sense of humor (he always makes me laugh), is very complimentary and kind, still says I am beautiful when I wake up in the morning and look like hell, and still says I am beautiful when I have gained fifteen pounds. He is always very kind to me; every woman needs this! And every man needs this, too; he is very hot and sexy to me, and I let him know it!

✦

- If you have children, you take the time to attend to each other as a couple and not just as parents.
- You communicate with each other out of care and concern instead of judgment and criticism.

Red Flags and Gut Feelings

Red flags in relationships are seriously unappealing or problematic actions, attitudes, and behaviors exhibited by your partner. These behaviors will trigger a response in your gut, an indication that something is not right in your relationship.

How can you recognize *your* red flags?

- Think about red flags for you. What red flags have you observed in past relationships? What about your current relationship? Write them down and reflect on them.

- Are you changing your behavior in response to your boyfriend or fiancé? Are you isolating yourself, avoiding your friends and family? Do you feel like you are walking on eggshells all the time? Be honest.

How can you connect your red flags to your gut feelings?

- Think about your gut feelings. How would you describe them? Is it a "little voice inside your head"? Is it a "feeling"? What do you call it? Intuition, a sixth sense, your conscience? Be aware of how *you* respond. Make a connection between the red flags and the gut feelings.

Part 2: How Not to Get Engaged to the Wrong Guy

Why do you want to get engaged?

Have you carefully considered the following?

• Are you racing to the altar? Why do you want to get married?

• Will you want to marry this man six months from now?

• Do you think that everything will be "perfect" once you are actually married?

• Do you believe that your life will be instantly and magically happier once you utter your vows?

• Do you think marriage is a way out of your current loneliness, dead-end job, or personal doldrums?

• Are you getting married just because you think it is the next logical step in your courtship?

• If you are engaged, do you think you are getting married for the wrong reasons? Be honest.

• Do you and your boyfriend/fiancé share the same goals, beliefs, and ideals for your marriage?

• Have you even *talked* about any of this with him?

Are you under pressure?

Are you feeling pressured by any of the following?

• Do your parents think it's time for you to get married?

• Do your parents want you to marry your longtime boyfriend?

• Are your friends encouraging you to get married?

• Are your friends all getting married, so you want to get married, too?

• Has the age that you always planned on getting married passed you by?

• Have you been dating the same person so long that you don't want to throw it all away, or feel like you have wasted that time?

• Is your biological clock ticking?

• Do you have it together in your work life but not in your personal life? Would marriage really solve this?

• Are you looking for financial security?

• Do you want to get out of your parents' house?

Understanding Cold Feet and Jitters

Cold feet: Fearfulness or timidity preventing the completion of a course of action.

Jitters: A feeling of fright or uneasiness.

How can I be sure?

Take this quick multiple choice test and find out.

Q. You are feeling nervous about your wedding. Which of the following best describes the source of your concerns?

a. Planning the wedding and reception
b. Giving up my life as a single woman
c. Giving up my life as a single women *and* the stress of planning the wedding and reception
d. My relationship with my fiancé

Your answer:__.

If you answered a, b, or c—it's probably just jitters. If you answered d, you most likely have cold feet. Now consider the following:

• What red flags are you seeing as the engagement and wedding plans progress? How are you feeling? What are your concerns? Are they related to the wedding planning or to the relationship?

• Imagine your life with him five years from now. How do you *really* see yourself? Will you be living an authentic life or will you just be pretending?

• Is he the wrong guy for you? Why or why not?

After working through these questions, how do you feel? Do you and your fiancé have permanent or temporary issues that are troubling you? Are you simply nervous, or do you have reservations that are preventing you from taking the next step . . . down the aisle? If you are still not sure, consider this: **If you could walk away right now and cancel the wedding, free of fear, free of guilt, free from embarrassment, and financially free, would you do it?**

Be honest. If you would, then this is not "normal prewedding jitters." You've got cold feet.

Part 3: How Not to Marry the Wrong Guy

He's popped the question. Did you say, "Yes, I'll marry you" for any of the following reasons?

• You don't want to let everyone down or hurt your fiancé's feelings.

• You are afraid that this will be your one and only chance to get married.

• You believe that you have invested too much time in the relationship, and you don't want to waste all that time spent together.

If you agreed to get married for *any* of these reasons, it's time to rethink your engagement.

Are you going to say "I do" for any of the following reasons?
• You are too caught up in the momentum of the wedding and think it's too late to call it off.
• You are afraid of publicly admitting a mistake and want to avoid the shame and embarrassment of canceling your wedding.
• The potential financial losses of canceling the wedding are preventing you from calling it off.

If you answered yes to even one of the above, you are headed down the aisle to disaster. The good news is that it's not too late to call it off!
• Write down the reasons you are forging ahead with your wedding plans.
• Are they similar to the reasons found in chapter 6? Are they temporary reasons? Do they make sense?

Part 4: How to Break Up with the Wrong Guy

Do you have the ability to stand alone?
Ask yourself the following:
• Are you able to stand alone or are you held back by fear?
• What fears are keeping you in the wrong relationship?

- Are you making bad decisions about your relationships because you don't want to be alone? Why don't you want to be alone?

- Are you limiting yourself by remaining in a relationship that does not feel right to you?

- Which of these objections resonates with you?

"I wanted to have kids before the age of thirty. If I break up with him, I might not have a chance to have children because I will be too old."

"I don't want to hurt him. He needs me."

"He is going to change. He was so great when we started dating; I know that person is still inside of him."

"All of the good guys are taken, and I am afraid no one better will come along."

"If it doesn't work out I can always get divorced."

"I can't financially support myself on my own."

You must resist the urge to fall back on these objections. Don't believe that you are better off with the wrong guy rather than being alone. Plant your feet firmly on the ground and tell yourself, "I can stand alone! I am ready to make good choices in my life!"

Do you have doubts about canceling the party or ending the relationship?

Many women knew they should end the relationship itself—but the party got in the way. Ask yourself:

1. What is stopping me from calling off my wedding?

2. Is my hesitation related to any of the following issues?

- Money spent on the dress, flowers, shoes, reception
- A feeling that it is too late to cancel the big party— being caught up in the momentum
- Embarrassment over telling my wedding party that the party's off (Quit picturing your friends in their taffeta bridesmaid dresses; they are your friends first!)
- Disappointing people who are excited about the wedding

These are all issues related to canceling a party. Don't let the party-planning issues muddy the waters.

Next ask yourself:

3. Deep down, do I really want to end the entire relationship?

4. If the answer is yes, make a list of all the reasons why.

What steps do you need to take to call off your wedding?

Step 1: Give yourself some time to just think about calling it off.

Step 2: Say the words out loud: "I want to call it off."

Step 3: Take action: The secret is to do *something*!

It's not too late! You can do this! It's time to put your happiness back in your own hands.

Part 5: How to Find the *Right* Guy

Go back and read through the quotes in chapter 9 about what a good marriage to the right guy is like. Can you picture yourself saying these things about your guy five, ten, even twenty years from now? Also revisit the advice from Father Jim and Pastor Joe. Perhaps visiting a religious adviser could help shed some light on the nature of your relationship.

Remember, marrying the right guy begins with you! We wish you much success in life and love.

Did you call it off? We want to hear from you!

✦

*A*s we said in the beginning of the book, we will consider the cancellation of any destined-for-disaster wedding a success story. The end of an engagement counts, too. We also hope that there are lots of bad boyfriends sent packing as a result of this book. If you call off your wedding or break up with your boyfriend after reading this book, please visit our website and tell us about it. We'd love to hear your story.

www.hownottomarrythewrongguy.com

With your permission, we'll use your story on our website or blog to help other women find the courage they need to follow their gut feelings. Just as the stories in this book helped you, *your* story can help someone, too.

Thank you so much for reading our book. We hope that you found the answers that you have been looking for.

Resources

✦

Recommendations for Further Reading

While conducting research for this book, we spent countless hours at the library, in bookstores, and on the Internet trying to increase our awareness of complicated relationship issues. If you enjoy reading as much as we do, we highly recommend the following books:

Behrendt, Greg, and Liz Tucillo. *He's Just Not That Into You: The No-Excuses Truth to Understanding Guys.* New York: Simon Spotlight Entertainment, 2004.

Bloch, Douglas. *Listening to Your Inner Voice: Discover the Truth Within You and Let It Guide Your Way.* Minneapolis: Comp-Care Publishers, 1991.

Branden, Nathaniel. *Honoring the Self: Personal Integrity and the Heroic Potentials of Human Nature.* Los Angeles: J. P. Tarcher, 1983.

Chodron, Pema. *The Places That Scare You: A Guide to Fearlessness in Difficult Times.* Boston: Shambhala, 2001.

Cooper, Robert K. *The Other 90%: How to Unlock Your Vast*

Untapped Potential for Leadership and Life. New York: Crown Business, 2001.

DeVries, Susan, Bobbie Wolgemuth, Robert Wolgemuth, and Mark DeVries. *The Most Important Year in a Woman's Life: What Every Bride Needs to Know / The Most Important Year in a Man's Life: What Every Groom Needs to Know.* Grand Rapids, Mich.: Zondervan, 2003.

Gigerenzer, Gerd. *Gut Feelings: The Intelligence of the Unconscious.* New York: Viking, 2007.

Gilbert, Elizabeth. *Eat, Pray, Love: One Woman's Search for Everything Across Italy, India, and Indonesia.* New York: Viking, 2006.

Gottman, John, and Nan Silver. *The Seven Principles for Making Marriage Work.* New York: Crown Publishers, 1999.

Kerner, Ian. *Be Honest—You're Not That Into Him Either: Raise Your Standards and Reach for the Love You Deserve.* New York: ReganBooks, 2005.

Lerner, Harriet Goldhor. *The Dance of Connection: How to Talk to Someone When You're Mad, Hurt, Scared, Frustrated, Insulted, Betrayed, or Desperate.* New York: Harper Collins, 2001.

Mayerson, Charlotte. *Goin' to the Chapel: Dreams of Love, Realities of Marriage.* New York: BasicBooks, 1996.

Paul, Pamela. *The Starter Marriage and the Future of Matrimony.* New York: Villard Books, 2002.

Safier, Rachel, with Wendy Roberts. *There Goes the Bride: Making Up Your Mind, Calling It Off and Moving On.* San Francisco: Jossey-Bass, 2003.

Stepp, Laura Sessions. *Unhooked: How Young Women Pursue Sex, Delay Love and Lose at Both.* New York: Riverhead Books, 2007.

Stern, Robin. *The Gaslight Effect: How to Spot and Survive the Hidden Manipulations Other People Use to Control Your Life.* New York: Morgan Road Books, 2007.

Tolle, Eckhart. *A New Earth: Awakening to Your Life's Purpose.* New York: Dutton/Penguin Group, 2005.

Wallerstein, Judith S., and Sandra Blakeslee. *The Good Marriage: How and Why Love Lasts.* New York: Warner Books, 1995.

Other Resources You May Find Helpful

www.coldfeetpress.com: Visit our blog for more information about relationship issues.

www.selfleadership.org: Visit this website to learn more about the Internal Family Systems (IFS) model. Dr. Richard Schwartz describes his model in simple terms as "a conceptual framework and practice for developing love for ourselves and each other." You can also search the database of therapists who practice IFS.

www.smartmarriages.com: This website for the Coalition for Marriage, Family and Couples Education is packed with helpful resources—and it's not just for married people. There are books, articles, quotes, and information on several different relationship courses. The recommended resources and courses are for *any* couple at *any* stage—dating, engaged, newlywed, and cohabiting. They also offer distance-learning options.

Suggested Resources for Finding a Therapist

The following websites can help you locate a therapist in your area. Refer back to chapter 8 for detailed information on finding a qualified therapist.

www.coldfeetpress.com: Jennifer Gauvain, coauthor, is a licensed clinical social worker in private practice in St. Louis, Missouri. She also consults via telephone and Skype. Contact her via the website for more information.

www.find-a-therapist.com: The largest online database of therapy providers.

www.psychologytoday.com: Click on "Find a Therapist."

Acknowledgments

✦

Special Thanks from Both of Us

We both would like to thank the following people who helped make the second edition of this book a reality. First, we must thank Nikki Furrer, proprietress of Pudd'nHead Books in Webster Groves, Missouri. You know what you did! (*wink, wink*) We are also grateful to our calm, cool, and insightful agent, Daniel Lazar, at Writers House. You are a man of few words, but when you speak—we listen! We are so glad we took your advice. And of course, we must thank our wonderful editor, Hallie Falquet, who was enthusiastic about this book from the start. Thanks for rushing it to press and for providing so many fabulous suggestions. You are truly the answer to our prayers. And finally, we must thank Tripp Frohlichstein of MediaMasters, Inc. (our guru), Chris Kuban of Chemistry Multimedia, and Todd Schumacher of Shoebox Media Creations who helped bring this book to life. We are so grateful for your help!

———

First of all, I must thank all of women whose interviews made this book possible. Without your stories, there would be no book. I know it was difficult for many of you to revisit these painful memories. Your willingness to do so anyway in the hopes of helping other people was truly inspiring. Words can't express my gratitude.

I feel slightly guilty for not putting my dear husband, Doug, on the top line. His support and encouragement for this project was beyond measure. I love you very much and am so happy I married the *right* guy. I also can't thank my three beautiful children, Buddy, Grace, and Ted, enough for their love and support. They put up with a lot of poorly-thought-out meals, unmade beds, and late nights. (It's here where I should probably acknowledge the Art of Entertaining and Schwan's frozen food delivery service!) Kids, I am sorry about all the times I shushed you and kicked you out of my office because I was "working on the book!" I am so proud and happy to be your mom.

Love and thanks go to my father, Jack Collins. Your example of what a good husband and father looks like surely stopped me from marrying the wrong guy. I am finally realizing the full measure of the sacrifices you made to raise two daughters and put them through private school and college. I love you! I am certain that my mother, on her heavenly perch somewhere, is aware of this book as well. She hasn't sent me my winning lottery numbers yet, but she did send me the title in a dream. Thanks, Mom! We miss you.

Of course, I must recognize my wonderful coauthor, Jennifer. I would not have been able to finish this book without you. I am so grateful for your support, your professional wisdom, and, *most* important, your friendship. You have so many wonderful qualities that balance out my own, shall we say "quirkier" ones. What a team. It was so awesome to have my own therapist on standby twenty-four hours a day. Aren't you glad we went to Starbucks that day! (Thanks, Mary Michalski!)

Thanks, too, to all of my friends who had to listen to me talk about this project for so many years, particularly the IC. I don't want to name names for fear of leaving anyone out. I do apologize for repeatedly sucking all of you into my "wedding vortex." I also appreciate those who forwarded my emails, surveys, and questionnaires. Thanks for helping me find such great stories. Many thanks go to my dear St. Joe friends who took the time to read and critique the book.

I want to give special credit to the fabulous faculty of St. Joseph's Academy in St. Louis, the place where I learned how to write. Any positive characteristics that I may have—that that I did not receive from my family— came from my four years at St. Joe. I particularly want to thank Santa Cuddihee, Mary Alice Hennessy, and Leah Preston for recognizing my abilities, even though I was not at the top of my class. I am an example of what St. Joe can do for an intelligent yet highly uninspired student. Thank you from the bottom of my ADD heart.

I gratefully acknowledge my four years at Loyola University in New Orleans. While I loved Loyola, I suspect it was my time spent in the taverns and bars of Uptown New Orleans that really taught me how to tell a story and conduct an interview!

I would also like to recognize my amazing editors and

copy editors. Leslie Gibson McCarthy—if it wasn't for your wise advice, this book would have been nothing more than a wordy sermon. Your insights put this project on the right track. You are an outstanding writer, and now it's your turn to write a book. Many thanks also go to Rebekah Matt, "defender of the content." You zeroed in on so many key issues and offered razor-sharp advice. I also appreciate Dave Brumfield's eagle eye. As I always say about you, still waters run deep!

I also offer thanks to my professional helpers who did their part to bring this book to market: Christine Frank, Shelley Dieterichs, Linda Rivard, and Nate Paul. If you need a book packager, a graphic designer, a photographer, or a Web designer, these are the people to call. I must also thank Jane "Mary Poppins" Tayon for her help and cheerleading. I am also grateful to Bobby Linkemer and the St. Louis Publishers Association.

I also promised to recognize my carpool: Grace, Teddy, Jack, Joel, Katelyn, and Danny. Thank you for not saying anything to me about wearing the same sweat suit every day or commenting about my hair standing straight up after long hours of writing. I really appreciate it.

Thanks go to my neighbors, the Timpes, for letting me sit by their pool and write. I also appreciate the staff of the Crestwood Starbucks for keeping "time on task" with countless venti whole milk lattes. And, finally, I must acknowledge my two office assistants, Monsieur Le Choi and Mr. Dingo. You two kept me company for hours on end. (Side note: Did you know that cats snore and dogs chase Frisbees in their dreams?)

This has been a wonderful, fulfilling project and I am so

thrilled to complete it. I hope you enjoy reading it. *Most important, I hope it stops a whole lot of women from marrying the wrong guys!*

—*Anne Milford*

First and foremost I want to thank the most important person in my life, my husband, Dan. Your love, your patience, and your support have pushed me through this process in ways I cannot describe. We go together like peas and carrots and I can honestly say that I have never questioned whether you are the right guy. I can't wait to see what new adventures lie ahead for us. Most important, I thank you for the gift of our children, Julia and Josh. What a surprise we had that day in the ultrasound room nine years ago! I have always known what a wonderful father you would be, and I am so grateful that the three of us have you in our life.

Julia and Josh, my number one fans! Thank you for not complaining too much when I had to work on this project. I am honored to be your mom and to spend time with you enjoying the things you love most, such as reading, swimming, bike riding, hiking, and geocaching. I know you don't always have clean socks to wear, but you have been there cheering me on the whole way. Julia, I love your personal motto, "Believe what you believe. Don't believe what you don't believe." I know I believe in the two of you!

Now on to you, Anne. It has been an awesome and wild ride with you since our chance meeting at the Crestwood Starbucks that cold December day. Our connection was instantaneous, and I am quite certain that we knew each other in a past life. I do not believe in coincidences, and it seems both of our paths have led us to this amazing accomplishment. You helped me uncover a creative part of myself that had been dormant for quite some time. I had forgotten about that nine-year-old girl who wrote her first story in the third grade. She is so thankful to be rediscovered! Writing this book was a huge surprise in my life, but an even better surprise is the friendship and partnership that was the ultimate end result. This is just the beginning for Cold Feet Press!

To my parents, Colleen Connelly and Bryan Nelson. I know the past thirteen-plus years have not always been easy. I hope that you can find a way to see through my eyes as you read my words. You may not have been "right" for each other, but I hope you have now found the happiness you were looking for. I am sure I speak for my brother, Sean, when I say we are glad that we are the results of your marriage.

I need to send a thank-you out to Dr. Richard Schwartz, founder of the Center for Self Leadership and the Internal Family Systems model. I have met you only a handful of times, but your work has had such an impact on both my professional and personal life. I am thrilled to share some of that work with the world through this book. Thanks also to my Level 1 IFS group, especially my training staff, Paul Ginter, Elizabeth Taubert, Mary DuParri, Mark Robinson, Marni Pearlman, and Uri Talmor. The birth of this book coincided with my training, and I am so grateful that it did; otherwise, my critical parts would have totally halted my progress. I still have to remind myself that "all parts are welcome!"

There are several other "characters" in my story that I need to mention who have had an incredible impact on my life. They say teachers are our unsung heroes. So to every teacher who has ever touched my life, thank you! However, the teacher who stands out most for me is my tenth-grade English teacher, Gail Egleston. Your no-nonsense attitude was exactly what I needed then, and it helped me develop the writing skills that I continue to use today. You may not remember, but you gave me a copy of *The Prophet* for graduation. Twenty years later I continue to treasure this gift. We even snuck in a quote! I hope you are enjoying retirement and can find some joy in knowing what an important part you played in my journey.

Two other very important teachers I would like to acknowledge are Dr. Ann Dell Duncan and Dr. Wells Hively. You saw potential in me even before I did so many moons ago. Your clinical expertise and insight helped mold me as a person and helped me become the therapist I am today.

To all of my friends and colleagues, there are too many of you to mention by name, but you know who you are. You support has been astonishing. You responded to my countless emails and questionnaires. You patiently listened to my ideas and offered suggestions of your own. Many of you even shared your own personal relationship stories for these very pages. I am truly blessed to have so many wonderful, wise, and authentic people in my life.

And finally, thank you to all of the woman whom I have never met or spoken to but who shared their stories in this book. Thank you for your courage to answer an email from a complete stranger in an effort to help so many other women who are facing the exact same challenges in their relationships. Your stories are the most powerful piece of information a reader will take away from this book. We really do believe that if you understand how to marry the wrong guy, you will know how to marry the right one.

—*Jennifer Gauvain*